COACHING BEGINNING BASKETBALL

JIM
PRUITT

CONTEMPORARY
BOOKS, INC.
CHICAGO

Library of Congress Cataloging in Publication Data

Pruitt, Jim.
      Coaching beginning basketball.

      Includes index.
      1. Basketball coaching.   2. School sports.
I. Title.
GV885.3.P78   1980   796.32′3′077   79-23445
ISBN 0-8092-7089-7
ISBN 0-8092-7088-9 pbk.

Photos courtesy of Enterprise School

Published by Contemporary Books, Inc.
180 North Michigan Avenue, Chicago, Illinois 60601
Manufactured in the United States of America
Library of Congress Catalog Card Number: 79-23445
International Standard Book Number: 0-8092-7089-7 (cloth)
                                    0-8092-7088-9 (paper)

Published simultaneously in Canada by
Beaverbooks
953 Dillingham Road
Pickering, Ontario L1W 1Z7
Canada

To Joanne who puts up with being a coach's wife

To Jennifer and Jason Pruitt, my favorite athletes

To the West Central Trojanettes whose talent made me appear successful

To Bill Kapperman who helped me get started

To Jim Uttecht who helped me keep going

To the Parker Lady Pheasants who make coaching worth it.

Contents

1

Introduction:
Here's Your Ticket

This manual contains a simple and effective program that will make you an adequate junior high school coach even if you have no basketball background. The demand for coaches has increased, forcing many untrained teachers to tackle a job that may seem too big for them. It isn't, though.

The author faced such a predicament four years ago. But today he has a 60–24 record, a .714 percentage. He has coached both boys and girls and has never had a losing season. Yet he never played basketball during his own school years and had no formal training as a coach. His record was the result of a crash course in fundamentals, consisting of days, weeks, and months of intensive study and observation.

Such an all-out effort will be unnecessary for those who apply the principles in this manual. This single source cuts through the deadwood, the frills, and the philosophizing to present a workable program, complete. It can be a life-saver for you!

The material is presented with sufficient clarity to benefit not only school coaches but also YMCA coaches, city recreation department coaches, and others. It will also provide more experienced coaches with many new drills, plays, and ideas guaranteed to strengthen any program. Players, too, will find the manual helpful, as it is full of the tips they need to play varsity ball.

2

Practices

Length of practices varies. Whatever the length you are allowed, use every minute. Know in advance exactly what drills you are going to run. Troublesome areas should be included in the plans for the next day's practice. The drills in this manual are easy to set up, and they are geared to accomplish specific goals in the shortest time possible. Use them.

Use different drills to keep interest high.

Don't allow horseplay. Basketball is fun in its own right. Horseplay quickly leads to sloppy playing habits and can cause injuries.

Stress the importance of getting to all practices. To make this point, I prepare a mimeographed handout listing valid and invalid excuses for missing practices. I distribute these at the first team meeting or practice.

Examples of valid reasons for missing practice: Move to Central America, die, call from the hospital, attend your wedding, break a leg, get caught in an elephant stampede.

Examples of invalid reasons for missing practice: Your second cousin's wedding, a runny nose, a jammed finger, an appointment that could be rescheduled, homework.

I blow the whistle often during practices to immediately correct errors or point out particularly good efforts. I do this less often later, particularly during scrimmages where continuity and transitions are important.

Explain everything—talking is *not* wasting time. It is important to follow the KISS principle: "Keep It Simple, Stupid!" Don't assume the kids know all about the game, its terminology, etc. Even when they do know something, repeat it often so that they won't forget it too soon.

Don't take a condescending attitude, however. Preface remarks with something like, "I'm

Waist rolls. The girls are demonstrating, in sequence from left to right, each part of this four-position exercise.

Calf stretchers ("frisking" exercise).

sure many of you know this, but . . . ," or "Just in case anyone has forgotten about . . . ," etc.

After the first day, allow time for shooting at every practice. No fancy offense will win a game if your players can't get the ball through the hoop. It is important to establish a correct shooting form in junior high. The kids will need much *supervised* practice to break bad habits and reinforce new ones.

Conditioning must be stressed the first six or seven practices. After that, fitness can be maintained primarily by scrimmaging.

Don't overdo tough drills the first two days. The kids' enthusiasm is crucial to speedy progress.

Even late in the season, fundamentals are of paramount importance. Don't neglect them.

Here is a schedule you can use for a 90-minute practice the first week; after that, base practices on areas your players need most work in. Many drills are included in this manual with the areas they are meant to strengthen.

FIRST DAY

Introductory talk on what is expected of players. Distribute handout on practice attendance (10 min.)

Loosening up. Stretching exercises are best to prevent injuries—20 toe touches, 10 four-count waist rolls, 10 situps, 30 jumping jacks (or sidestraddle hops) (5 min.)

Jogging. Great for leg strength and wind. Preferably jog outside on gravel or dirt, as pavement or hard floors may cause shin splints (aching between knee and foot) (15 min.)

Stretching exercises (called "warmdown" in track). Lean against wall, as if being "frisked," feet shoulder width apart and flat on floor four or five feet away from wall; slowly rise to toes, down, rise, etc.

Hurdler's stretches. Sit on floor with legs at right angles, one to side and one straight ahead; grab toes without bending at knee, and hold for a few seconds each time; after a few repetitions switch legs (5 min.)

Hurdler's stretches. Not everyone will be able to stretch out as far as Gina does in this illustration!

Pivots (see Chapter 3) (10 min.)

Ball handling drills (see Chapter 4) (10 min.)

Dribbling (see Diagram 2–1) (10 min.)

Passes—chest and bounce pass (see Chapter 5) (10 min.)

Two-on-two. This is two players going against two others in a mini-game. It gives you a chance to preview them (15 min.)

SECOND DAY

Loosen up—ball handling and stretching exercises (5 min.)

Athletic stance and *shuffle* (see Chapter 9) (10 min.)

Layups (see Chapter 6) (15 min.)

Fakes with *passes* (10 min.)

Jogging (15 min.)

Stretching (5 min.)

Shooting (15 min.)

Pivots (5 min.)

Weave (Diagram 2–2) (10 min.)

THIRD DAY

Loosening up (5 min.)

Conditioning—ladders (Diagram 2–3) (5 min.)

Defensive shuffle (10 min.)

Layups (20 min.)

Jogging (20 min.)

Double fakes (10 min.)

Pivots (5 min.)

Dribbling. Races using each hand (10 min.)

Conditioning (5 min.)

FOURTH DAY

Warmups (5 min.)

Conditioning. Line drills (ladders) (5 min.)

Layups—left and right hand (10 min.)

Jogging (15 min.)

Head fakes (5 min.)

Pivots (5 min.)

Defensive positioning (see Chapter 9)   (10 min.)

Free throw shooting   (15 min.)

King-of-the-circle drill (Diagram 2–4)   (10 min.)

Rebounding   (10 min.)

FIFTH DAY

Warmups   (5 min.)

Conditioning. Line drills   (5 min.)

Layups. Left and right handed   (10 min.)

Free throws. Begin keeping daily record of shots made   (15 min.)

Jump shots   (15 min.)

Pivots   (5 min.)

Passing. Lob passes upcourt (baseball pass)   (10 min.)

Conditioning. Calisthenics   (5 min.)

Rebounding   (10 min.)

Defense. Protecting the baseline   (10 min.)

We begin working on an offensive pattern the second week. After the players have learned two plays, we start having scrimmages every practice unless the next day is a game day. Also, during the second week players must learn the basic man-to-man defense to make scrimmaging more beneficial.

It is best to schedule games as early as possible so players know what teams they're playing in advance. It helps keep enthusiasm up. It is wise to call the opposing coach the day before a game to make sure his team will show up and to find out whether they will be wearing light or dark uniforms and for which grade if they differ.

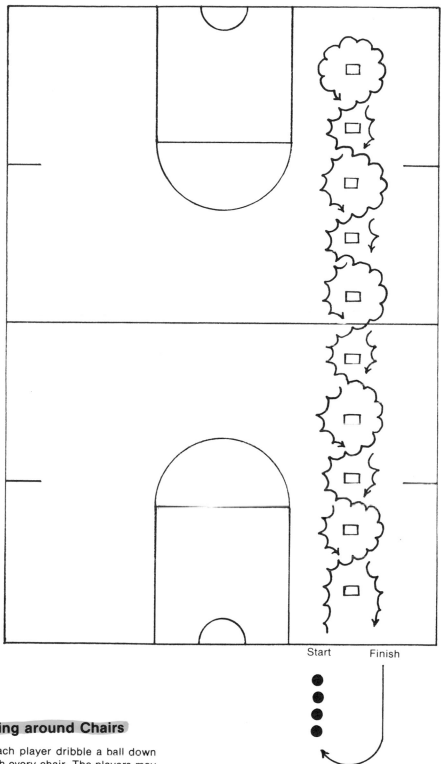

Start   Finish

Diagram 2-1. Dribbling around Chairs

Set up chairs, and have each player dribble a ball down the line, changing angles with every chair. The players may return down the same line of chairs or another line may be set on the opposite side of the court so that seven or eight players can dribble at once.

I like to use the one line only and let several players go at once, so that they have to watch out for each other. This forces them to keep their heads up more and change dribble speed. Tell players each chair is a defensive man, and they must keep the ball on the protected side of their body.

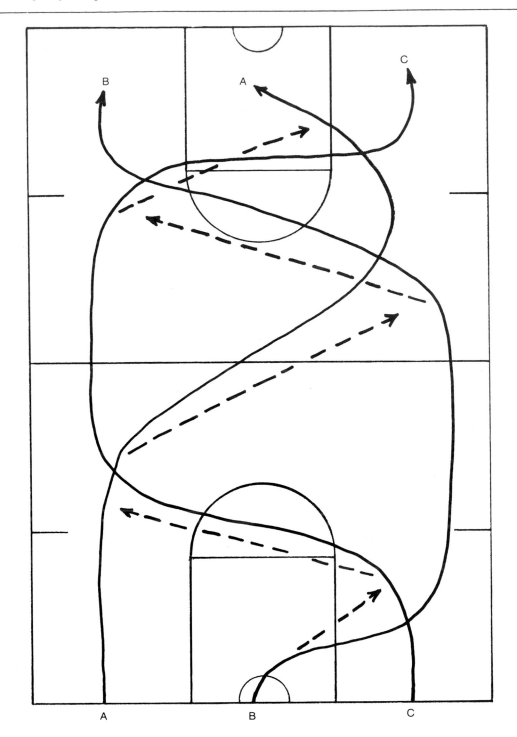

Diagram 2-2. Three-man Weave

Each person passes to the player on the side and goes behind him to continue up that side until he receives another pass, which he returns to the opposite side and goes behind the receiver, etc.

Five passes should be enough if the players are moving forward continuously unless they stop to wait for a pass or make one too low or behind someone.

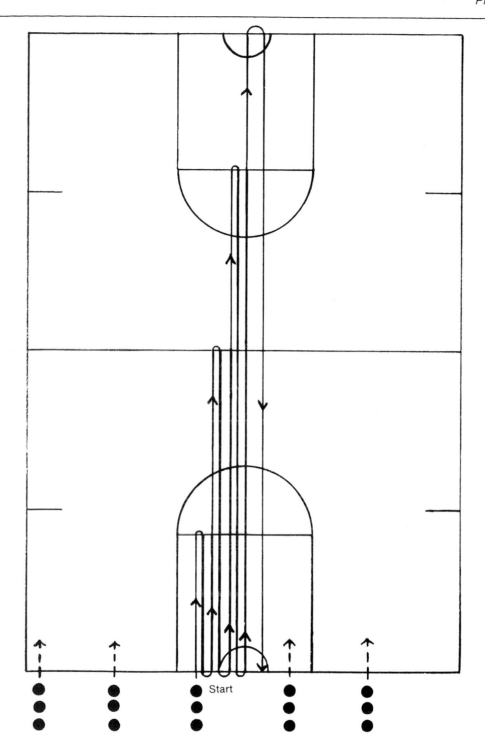

Diagram 2-3. Ladders or Line Drill

The movements of one player are diagramed but seven or eight may go at once. The players must go from the endline (i.e., baseline) to each successive line starting with the free throw line and back again, then to the next farthest line and back, etc. They may do this gliding or shuffling sideways in an athletic stance or crouch. They may sprint forward to each line and run backward to the starting point each time and may be required to touch each line with the hand.

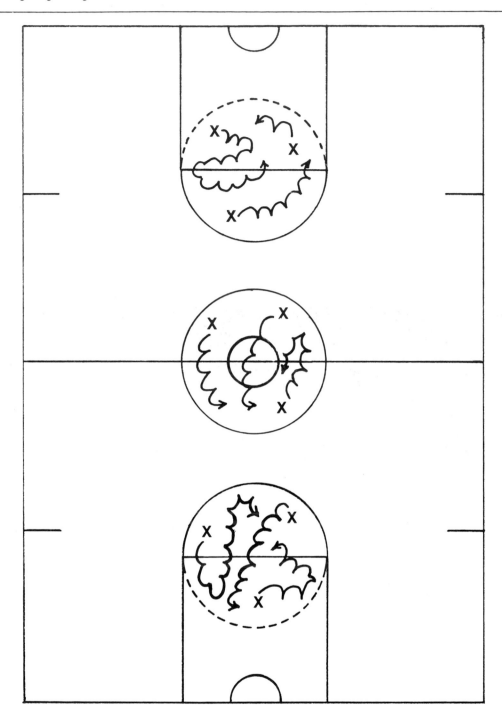

Diagram 2-4.   King of the Circle

Each of the two to four dribblers in each circle must dribble continuously while trying to bat away the ball dribbled by the other players. Breaking, i.e., stopping the dribble, stepping or dribbling outside the circle, or allowing the ball to be batted away, all result in the offender's dropping out. The drill may be run as a tournament, with the winners of each threesome or foursome being sent back in against each other until one player has won.

3

Pivots, Fakes, Driving Lane

PIVOTS

Few players reach junior high school age with any knowledge of what a pivot is or how to execute it. Yet this simple move is basic to any team's offense. It is the only way to maneuver around a good defensive player once the dribble has been used, to name just one of its functions.

Have players stand with their feet shoulder-width apart, knees bent, weight on the balls of the feet. Tell them one toe is nailed to the floor. They may move only by swinging around—pivoting—with the weight on the pivot ("nailed") foot during each turn. Moving the pivot foot any other way is a traveling violation.

The free foot should be swung in a direction away from the defender, so the ball is protected by being shielded from the defender with the body. This doesn't mean a player who is dribbling should start backing into the defense—

little can be done offensively that way. However, after a dribble when attempting to line up a passer with a safe target, a good pivot places the nearest defender safely behind the ball carrier.

The usual problem with pivoting is balance. Because players get off-balance at first, they are afraid to pivot when they should. Only daily drills can give them the confidence they need until this maneuver becomes automatic. Several good drills are provided in this chapter.

FAKES

Another simple but often unused method of getting clear for offensive positioning is the fake. Fakes should be used before passing, driving in, or shooting, and to get clear to receive a pass.

No. 55 has taken a rebound with a defensive player nearby.

The rebounder has pivoted away from the defensive player and can safely outlet to Number 21.

A single fake means the player pretends to be starting off in one direction and then goes the opposite way. The move must be quick but very definite—a halfhearted, sluggish gesture in one direction won't fool anybody. Once a strong fake is made, the player must go immediately the other way—a pause will allow the defender to recover and stay with the person who faked.

A double fake gets the defender off-balance and unable to go anywhere for a few moments. It is a single fake one way, then a single fake the opposite way, then a move back in the direction of the first fake just as the defender is recovering from the first fake and starting back the other way. Double fakes set up the use of single fakes and keep a defender more tense, tiring him and causing him to hesitate continually as well.

A head fake is often effective to get the defender to leave his feet attempting to stop a shot that isn't actually taken until the leaping defender has hit the peak of his jump and started back down. Of course, it is completely impossible to do anything about stopping the actual shot because the players are going in opposite directions. The head fake is a straightening movement upward, pulling not only the head but the shoulders sharply upward as if jumping, without leaving the floor.

All fakes may be defended against most effectively by a player who is disciplined enough to watch the beltline, or stomach and waist area, of the person faking. During a fake this part of the body remains stationary. When the middle of the torso moves, the defender should go with it, knowing that movement is genuine. Such defense must be constantly practiced.

DRIVING LANE

Driving around a defender is easiest when he has foolishly taken himself out of defensive position by lunging in an attempt to steal or bat down the ball. When the defender has thus committed himself, it is an opportunity for the dribbler to speed past him before he can stop and reverse direction again.

Even when a defender does not make such an amateurish move, it may be possible to get a step on him and go around if he is guarding too closely. Overguarding an opponent does not allow a player the time he needs to adjust to that opponent's moves. A player should stay back on defense, holding his position, until the offensive player has used his dribble; then it is safe to crowd him, since he can't go around.

If a defender is in position but is not totally stationary, a good ball handler can move steadily forward, backing the defender up. This is called driving in. The player must not push into the defender with an elbow or a lowered shoulder, however, or he is committing a charging violation. Otherwise, it is almost always the defender who is called for a foul if contact occurs. Against a good drive, a defender will either foul or step sideways out of the way.

It is not safe to drive into more than one defender at a time. It is too easy to trip, and this

The dribbler has faked a drive to her left and now dribbles around the defensive player to the right. The defensive player has been incorrectly watching the ball handler's eyes instead of her midsection, which has caused her to be easily faked out of a good defensive position.

can result in a traveling call or at least loss of control. Guards in particular should become skilled at knowing just when to drive or stop.

Against a full-court press, an aggressive guard is valuable because he will usually get the ball advanced over the center line within the ten seconds allowed.

One way to stop a driving opponent is to get far enough in front so that the defensive position is clearly established as the defender stops. Also some blocking with the chest is usually overlooked by the referee.

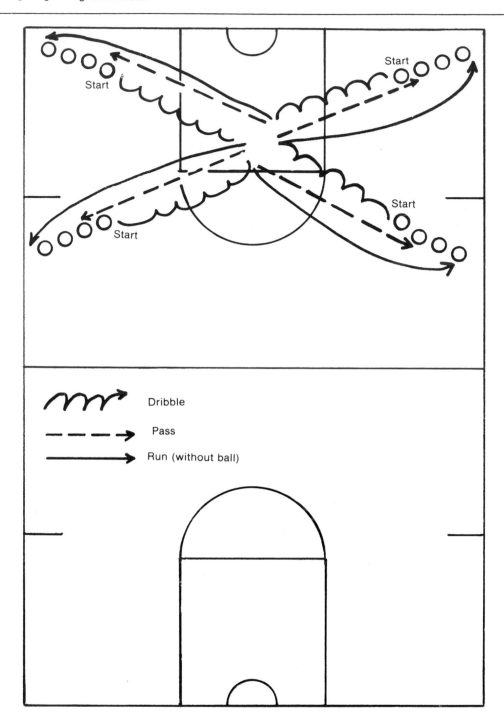

Dribble

Pass

Run (without ball)

Diagram 3-1.   Pivot-Pass Drill

Each player at the front of the line has a ball. The players dribble to the center point, make a half-pivot, and, facing the next player in the line originally to their right, fire the ball to that player and follow the pass to take a place at the end of the next line. After a time, change the direction and have players pivot and pass to the line on their left.

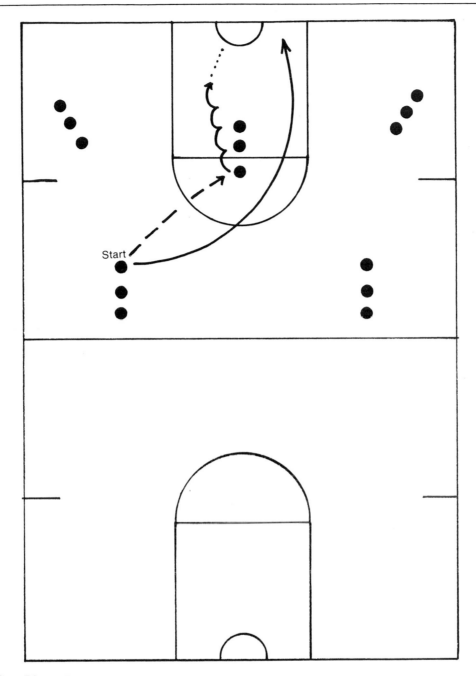

Diagram 3-2. Pivot Drill from Offensive Formation

This drill is helpful to teach centers to roll in for a shot after receiving a pass, and also it teaches other players to go with their pass.

The pass may be initiated from any of the four outside positions in to the center. The passer follows quickly, cutting by the receiving center into the lane. The center fakes a handoff one way to the passer, then pivots and dribbles in for a shot. Each player returns to a line: guards to one of the guard lines, centers to the centers' line, and forward to one of the forwards' lines. The center rebounds his own shot and quickly passes the ball out to any of the four outside positions to set up the next sequence. (......... = shot)

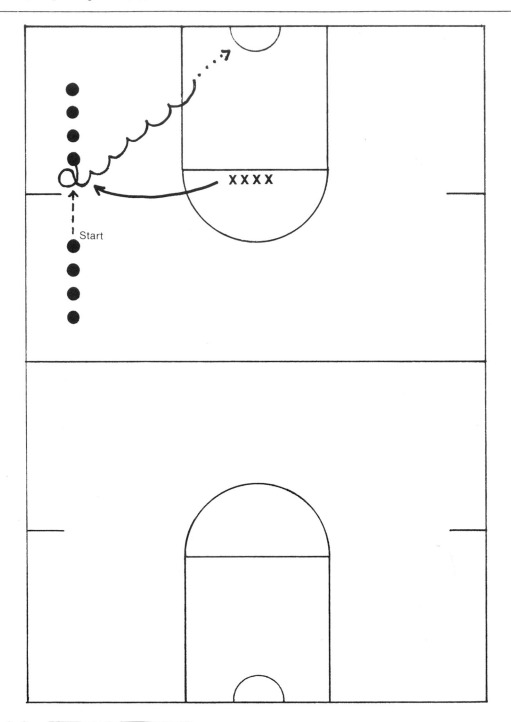

Diagram 3-3. Pivot and Score Drill

The pass goes to the player moving in the direction of the pass. As the ball comes to him, the player stops, pivots away from the defensive player (X) who has moved into position from the side, and after the pivot the player dribbles in quickly and takes the shot. The shooter then goes to the defensive line; the defender goes to the passing line; and the passer goes to the shooting line.

This drill stresses moving into the pass. This movement is absolutely essential to complete passes. A player who stands in one spot waiting for the ball will cause many passes to be picked off easily by the defense.

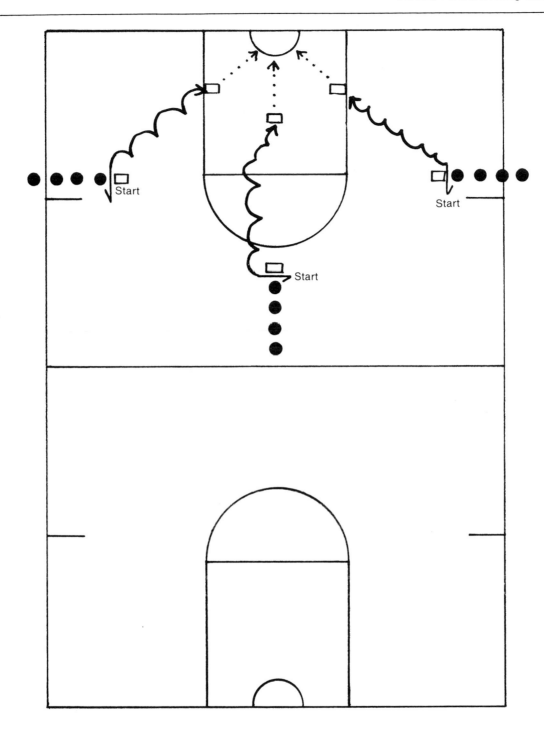

Diagram 3–4.   Fake 'em-Outta-Their-Shoes Drill

Each player faces chairs representing the defense. With a strong fake one way, a player rolls around the opposite side, dribbles up to the next chair, stops abruptly, gives a head fake, and shoots. After retrieving the ball, each player goes to a different line.

4

Dribbling and Ball Handling

Discourage excessive and pointless dribbling. A dribble is used only to advance the ball (as in a drive to score), to buy time until someone is open, or to escape pressure and get free enough to pass the ball. Otherwise, it may be used in a stall or delay game. But remember dribbling in most situations merely increases the odds for a turnover. Remind players often that passing is the best way to move the ball because it is faster and, especially with younger players, safer.

The most important point to stress about dribbling is to keep the head up. It is impossible for a player to see when other players are open or defenders are closing in when he has his nose glued to that ball. I have a drill for inexperienced players to keep their heads up by dribbling the length of the court and back, calling out the number of fingers I hold up as I retreat backwards in front of them. Another way is the two-ball dribble, also good for developing ball handling skill. In this drill the player must dribble two balls at once, racing in a team relay situation. It forces him to go by the feel of the ball since it is hard to look directly at both simultaneously. It also helps start players dribbling with their weak (usually left) hand.

In control dribbling the objective is not speed but control for deceptive movement. Therefore, the ball should be kept low. I have players dribble while trying to keep the ball only knee high during the first few days. On a speed dribble, such as when a player has the ball out in front of the defense and is hurrying to score, the ball is often overrun. So it is important to have some competitions early in the season to teach players in this situation to push the ball well out in front and catch up to it, rather than dribble with shorter, quicker strokes. Emphasize smoothness and tell players that it is better to risk being overtaken and having to set up the regular offense than to lose the ball by kicking it away.

Many young players want to back into the defense. They cannot see enough of the court this way. Teach them to protect the dribble by dribbling more to one side while facing forward. Dribbling at the side incurs less risk of getting in the way with one's own body, anyway. One reason players tend to keep the ball in front of them is to watch it, which has already been mentioned as a serious fundamental mistake.

Ball-handling exercises are essential in the grade school years. Players must become so used to the feel of the ball that they need to give it hardly any more thought than wearing gloves. Otherwise, they are uncomfortable and nervous whenever they handle the ball. The best way for them to get used to the feel of the ball is to handle it constantly, not just in practice but at home as well. I tell players to dribble while eating, bounce the ball beside the bath tub, etc. Of course, this is an exaggeration, but exaggerating is helpful to make some points memorable to a young player. Some basic ball-handling exercises follow.

TIPPLING

Without grabbing the ball, a player flips it back and forth with the fingers, arms outstretched at right angles from the body. Gradually the arms are raised as the tippling continues, until the ball is up over the head. It is then slowly lowered again.

MONKEY DRILL

A leader (one of the team captains or the coach) faces the group. They must watch him and do as he does. He dribbles the ball, switching hands, going between the legs in a figure eight, switching directions, etc. He may also pass the ball around and around the body at the waist, neck, and then up overhead.

CRADLES

The ball is held between the legs, right hand on the ball in front of the legs, left hand on the

As he goes to his left, the dribbler is wisely using his left hand to keep his body between the ball and the defensive man.

Here the dribbler is incorrectly attempting to protect the ball by pushing off the defensive player—an offensive foul.

ball behind the legs. Then, releasing the ball, the player quickly reverses the arm position, grabbing it with right hand behind and left in front. Some who have not done this will have a terrible time of it at first. But don't give up on them, and don't let them give up on themselves. They will surprise themselves and you sooner or later by suddenly catching on.

CLAP-AND-CATCH

Hold the ball straight out in front or against the body at waist level. Release, clap the hands behind the back, and grab the ball again before it touches the floor. This and other drills in this section increase quickness and confidence.

FIGURE EIGHT

Pass the ball from hand to hand between the legs in a figure-eight pattern. Then, as this gets easier, a player can walk while moving the ball in the same way, and eventually he will even be able to run while doing it.

HIKE DRILL

Bounce the ball backward between the legs, reach around, bending down, and catch it behind the legs. Then bounce it back again, forward, catching it once again in front, in the original position.

WALKING DRIBBLE

Beginning with one leg forward, bounce the ball between the legs. Continue bouncing it as you walk forward, pushing it between the legs each time.

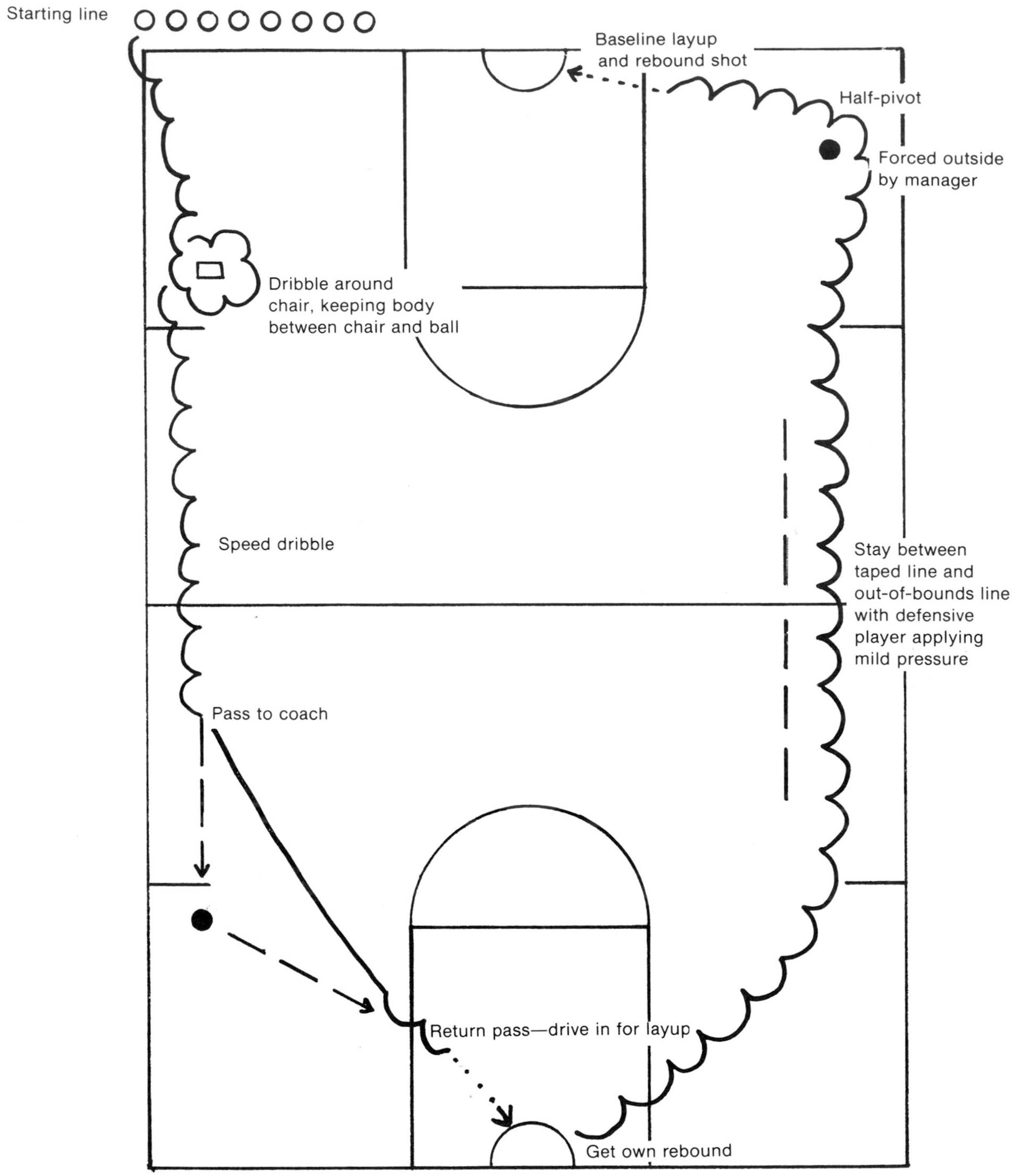

Starting line   O O O O O O O

Baseline layup
and rebound shot

Half-pivot

Forced outside
by manager

Dribble around
chair, keeping body
between chair and ball

Speed dribble

Stay between
taped line and
out-of-bounds line
with defensive
player applying
mild pressure

Pass to coach

Return pass—drive in for layup

Get own rebound

Diagram 4-1.   Obstacle Course

This drill may be timed. Start calling off the time at the first player's movement; each successive player goes at five-second intervals and listens for the time as he makes the layup upon returning to the starting point.

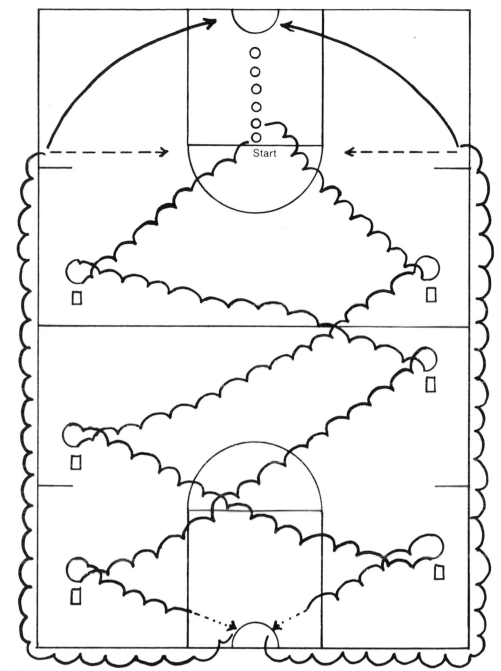

Start

Diagram 4-2. Dribble and Pivot Race

Teams line up in alternating order (or two lines side by side). Each player dribbles to a chair, pivots in the direction away from it, continues to the next chair, pivots, etc., until a shot can be taken in the lane. Then he must sprint along the sideline to give the ball to the next player, passing it to him when he arrives at a point where the free throw line would intersect if extended.

Players can be used to stand where chairs are shown on the diagram, to get the drill set up sooner.

Players must keep their heads up to avoid collisions with the other dribbler. Each should go twice, once in each direction, which means some players may need to get around a slower dribbler from the other team still going that way.

5

Passing

Young players often force passes by trying to hit a player who perhaps should be open according to the plan, but isn't. They also panic-pass, which means they throw the ball almost anywhere in an effort to get rid of it, hoping a teammate will snare it and make things come out all right. Talk to them about this. They must control such tendencies by never panicking.

Passes must be crisply thrown, except for lobs over the defense to a tall or wide-open player. Lazy passes are the number one cause of interceptions.

A good fake will avoid interceptions by the player defensing the passer as well as the receiver. Work hard on them.

The receiver must always move forward into the pass. Then another player attempting to intercept cannot do so without fouling. The receiver must watch the ball into his hands, then move. Still another way to avoid interceptions is to vary the types of passes used.

CHEST PASS

This is the standard basketball pass. It is easiest to get off quickly. The player steps in the direction he is passing and reaches out after his pass, following through so the thumbs end up in a downward position. Initially, the fingers of each hand are on the sides of the ball pointing at the target, and the thumbs are slightly behind the ball. Fingers should be spread, but not like claws, just slightly more than when the hands are dangling completely limp.

BOUNCE PASS

Hit a point just over halfway to the target so the ball bounces up to the receiver's middle.

Chest pass. Sandra reaches after her pass, thumbs turning downward from the wrist snap used to execute the maneuver. To receive the pass, Marcia has stepped toward it and has begun to reach for it, which is safer than waiting for it to reach her.

This is like a chest pass: The hand position is the same, but a follow-through is needed.

This is a particularly useful pass against a much taller man or into the lane area, where there is more room between the tangle of legs than higher up where bodies present wider obstructions; also in the lane a good defensive player will have his arms raised. In addition, a bounce pass is easier for the receiver to control quickly enough to get off a shot.

OVERHEAD PASS

Against a shorter opponent or one with lowered arms, a passer may reach or jump straight up and flip the ball over to the receiver. On a jump pass, a shot may be faked; the defender will rarely be able to deflect the pass since he is expecting the ball to go upward, not downward.

LOB OR BASEBALL PASS

This is thrown from behind the passer's upper body, one-handed, like a baseball or heavy stone. It is used exclusively to hit a wide-open player much farther upcourt. We find it is best to put some arc on the pass or even allow it to bounce behind the receiver, because younger players find it difficult to control bullet passes at a great distance.

LOOKAWAY PASS

Using the peripheral, or side, vision, the passer snaps the ball to a nearby teammate. A defender who is watching the passer's eyes or body position cannot tell where this pass is going, and it also allows the passer to break more quickly in the opposite direction of his

Bounce pass. As in the chest pass, the passer takes a step toward her target and reaches after her pass.

The bounce pass should contact the floor approximately two-thirds of the way to the target so it will bound toward the receiver's midsection.

Overhead pass. The ball is correctly flipped with two hands, over the head of the shorter defensive man.

Here the overhead pass is too high; if it does not drop down perfectly to the intended receiver, any nearby defensive player has time to knock it away or intercept. By jumping, the passer could launch the ball on a flatter trajectory.

Lob or baseball pass. For more power and accuracy in passing to an open teammate a great distance away, the ball is drawn back behind the ear and thrown one-handed, much like a fielder throws a baseball.

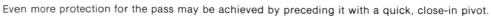

Reacharound pass. The passer's hands are past the crowding defender, so the pass will be completed safely.

Even more protection for the pass may be achieved by preceding it with a quick, close-in pivot.

pass. When a defender is reacting instinctively, leaning in the direction the ball went, the passer easily speeds around him and may take a return pass for a score.

REACHAROUND PASS

When being guarded too closely by an opponent, a player may reach around him and bounce or flip the ball to a receiver. The defender is unable to stop the pass because of his position, and if he does he will hit the passer's arm, fouling him.

There are other types of passes, but it is best to learn the basic ones well and to let such showy maneuvers as the behind-the-back pass go until college.

Stress to all players than anyone close must help out any passer who is in trouble and cannot get a pass off. This is done by either getting clear of one's own defender and calling to the passer to let him know he has help, or by speeding around behind him so when he hears the call he can pivot away from the trouble and safely hand off to the receiver. However, it does more harm than good if everyone heads in the direction of the passer, because they only draw more defenders into the area. Only the closest player should go around behind.

It is dangerous to pass upcourt too far with opponents near the potential receiver. It is also dangerous to pass across the lane unless a player is completely open there. The safest passes are short ones to the most open players, without going over other players and their defenders.

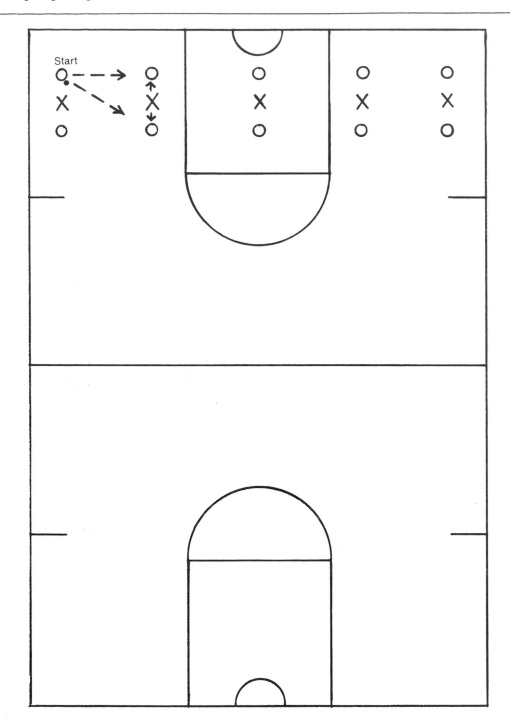

Diagram 5-1.   Hit the Open Man

Os must get the ball from one end of the line to the other. Each man may pass to either of the men facing each other next in line. The Xs may guard either of the pair next in line, so the Os must quickly find the open player. We consider it a turnover if the ball is held for two seconds.

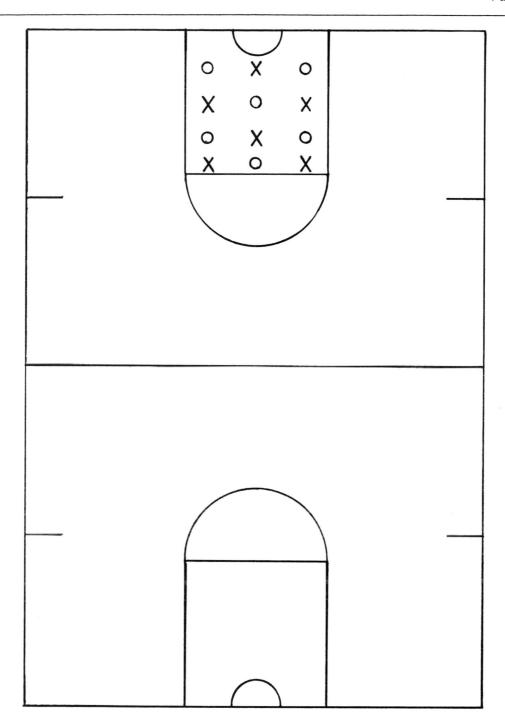

Diagram 5-2. Keep the Ball Drill

The more the merrier in this drill—more floor space can be used. One side has the ball. On the whistle, they must pass the ball around. They can pass to anyone. The opponents may take a step in any direction to intercept, or they may jump upward. When the ball is intercepted or even touched, the other side takes it to try completing a greater number of passes. Kids thrive on this sort of competitive drill.

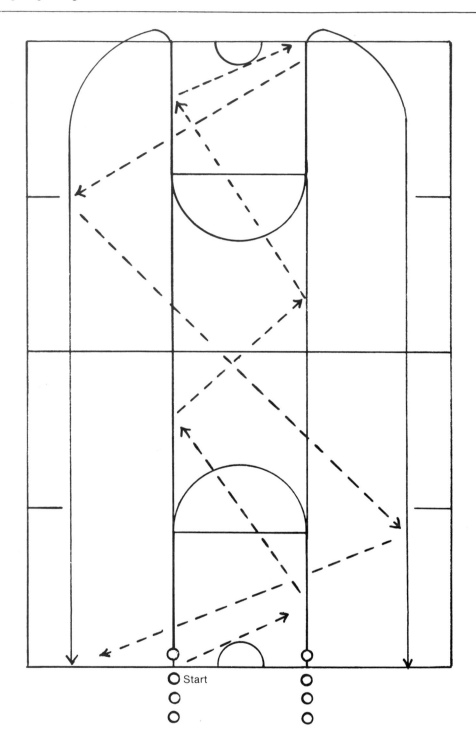

Diagram 5-3. Long and Short Drill

Two players pass the ball back and forth without dribbling or traveling. When they reach the end, they start back on the outside, making longer passes.

As each pair gets past the free throw line, the next pair starts, so passes must be accurate. Concentration is required to stay clear of other pairs, particularly when passing over inside pairs from outside to outside.

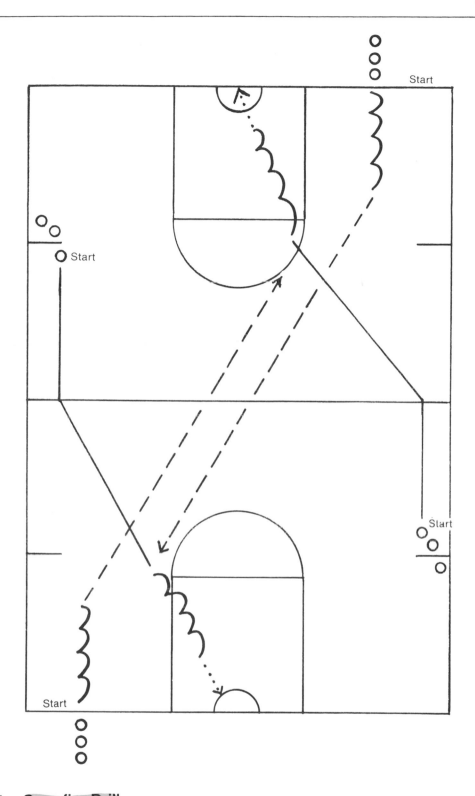

Diagram 5-4.   Crossfire Drill

The players at the endlines each have a ball. They dribble out and pass upcourt to the player breaking in from the opposite sideline as that player nears the lane. The receiver takes one or two dribbles as necessary and shoots a layup. Dribblers must concentrate to avoid dribbling or passing into the other receiver.

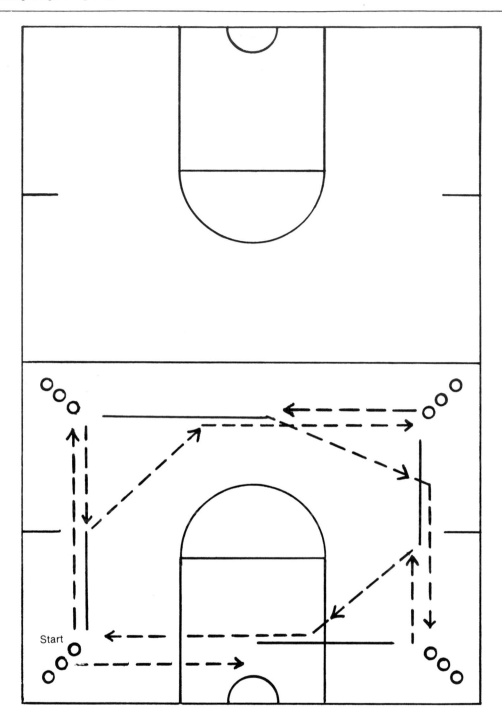

Diagram 5-5. Corner Route Drill

The player with the ball passes to the corner ahead of him and follows his pass. The receiver passes back to him and breaks toward the next corner clockwise. The first player once again passes to his original receiver and goes to the end of that player's line.

Now the second player follows the same procedure with the player at the head of the line he has started for.

After the drill is going well, use two balls, starting them at opposite corners.

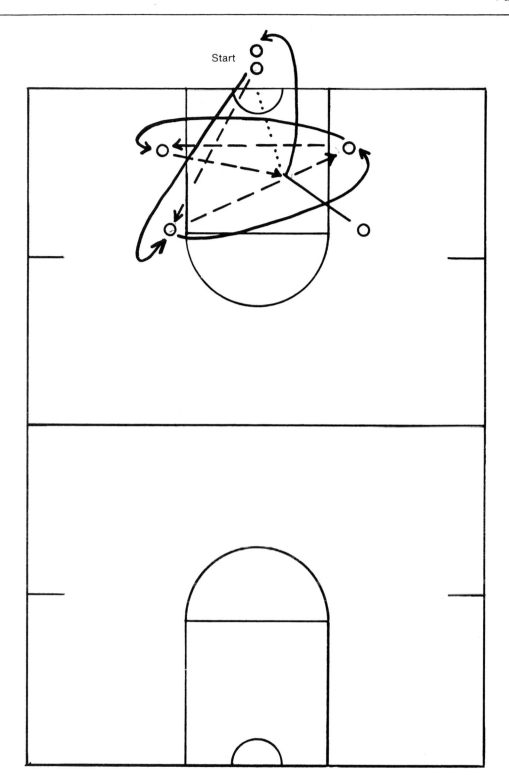

Diagram 5-6. Star Drill

The player at the baseline passes to a far corner and follows his pass. His receiver passes to the opposite corner and follows the pass. That receiver passes across the lane to a player who hits the man in the far corner from him for the layup. The shooter replaces the rebounder under the basket and starts the ball around again.

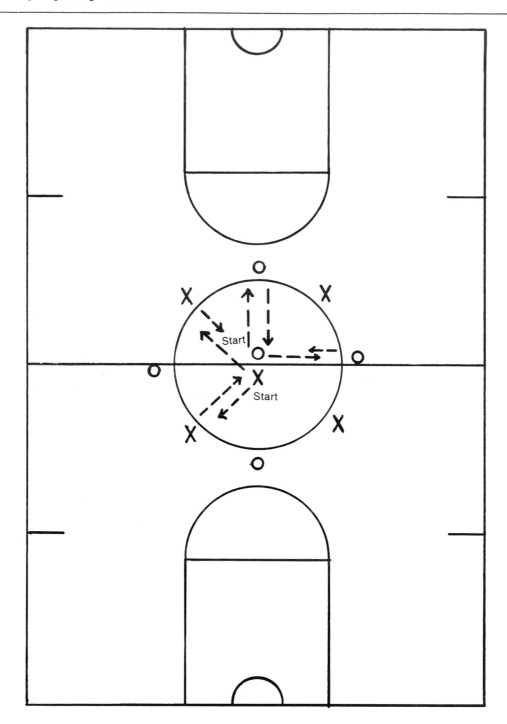

Diagram 5-7.   Catchup Drill

This is a contest between the Xs and Os. The man in the center passes to his teammate and receives a quick return pass. He then passes to the next player on his side. The rotation continues as rapidly as possible with each side attempting to catch up and pass the other. The side which does so wins.

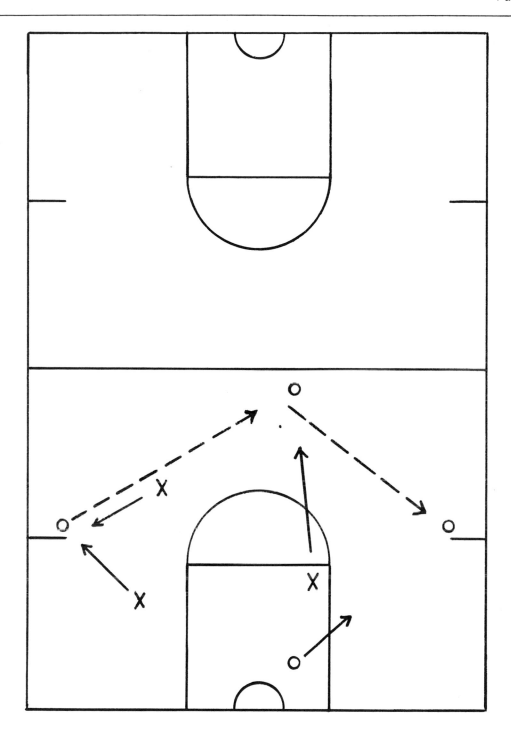

Diagram 5-8.   Wild Bull Drill

The Xs are wild bulls. They may do anything short of injuring an opposing player. Since there are four Os, they should be able to pass the ball around quickly before a "wild bull" can grab them or shove them. When a pass is touched, the bull goes on offense and a new bull comes in.

6

Shooting

Many youngsters are just reaching the point when they have enough arm and wrist strength to execute a proper shot. Until they have this strength, they tend to shoot a push shot from the chest or stomach area, often twisting the body for added force. It is time to correct this shot in junior high school. Some balking often occurs, because the correct method will not score as often at first as will the incorrect shot which the youngster has used much longer and has grown comfortable with. Inform players that eventually they will regain and surpass their present percentage, and besides, a push shot will be impossible for them to get off successfully against taller players and players who have learned to play defense. You will have to keep after the players constantly about shooting properly for as long as the first half of the season, in some cases. They may want to shoot as they are taught, but it is easy to slide back to the old way without insistent supervisory efforts on your part.

I teach layups before jump shots, because learning to reach up at the bankboard helps lead in to the elevation of the ball on jumps. Also, even against a zone, a good team will shoot more layups than anything else.

LAYUPS

The layup is just what the name implies—laying the ball up, not shooting it up. The bodily momentum carries the ball upward from the point of release. Teach your players that a layup comes off a high jump, not a long jump. They must try to shoot themselves upward from a point fairly close to the basket.

The layup is shot off the opposite foot from the shooting hand. This allows for greatest upward extension and control. Thus, layups from the right-hand side are off an upward jump from the left, or inside (basket-side) foot, and on the left-hand side the shooter goes off the right foot, shooting with the left hand.

It may help players to think of the layup as almost a two-handed shot: The ball should be carried upward with the support hand still on it until the last instant when the ball is released. Otherwise, players want to shoot a sort of half-hook, releasing the ball shoulder high or head high and from a point outside. It should be shot with the arms up in front of the player's head. One way to express the desired release is to tell players to stay with the shot longer.

A player must always use the bankboard on a layup if there is any angle at all. Even on a layup shot from directly in front of the basket, most players hit the bankboard over and behind the basket and let it ricochet in.

Watch for twisting of the body. The player should get the shoulders square to the target before the release.

The most important point of all is to keep the head up, to find the basket; otherwise, a player will start the shot too far out or get underneath so far that it's almost impossible to do anything but slam the ball into the underside of the rim or bankboard. I tell my players that I'd much rather see them lose the dribble on the way in than look down at it. Better control will only come from continuing to try the shot correctly, with the eyes up.

Another common flaw is lack of bodily control due to racing in too fast. Even in games when fastbreaking, a player is better off going too slowly than too fast. The worst that will happen is that the ball will be knocked away out of bounds by a faster opponent—but then the team still has possession of the ball. More often, an overtaking opponent will draw a foul. On the other hand, going too fast very often results in a player's losing control and fumbling or kicking the ball out of bounds himself, which causes his team to lose the ball. Too much speed also sharply decreases a player's chances of making the shot, and then an approaching opponent usually gets the rebound. Again, no score and no ball!

Players should shoot layups every day. We have races, go against time, and play a game in which the pair racing may tap each other's dribble or missed shot away to get an edge.

JUMP SHOT

Here are some points to emphasize. Elevate the ball, shooting it from overhead with the

Layup. Cathy has kept her left (supporting) hand on the ball almost until the release. The shot is taken with her arms in front of her, and she is jumping off her left (inside) foot.

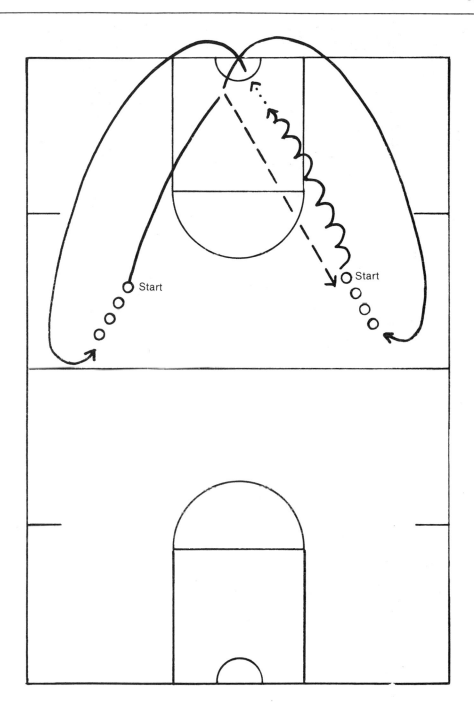

Diagram 6–1. Standard Layup Drill

This is the most-used drill for practicing layups. The players are in two lines. One line rebounds, the other drives in with the ball and shoots. The rebounder passes to the next player in the shooting line and takes a place in that line while the player who shot goes to the end of the rebound line. After a few minutes, players reverse lines and shoot layups on the left side. Left-handed layups are almost impossible for youngsters who have not tried them. But any junior high school player can learn to shoot one correctly the first year, and it is a must for high school.

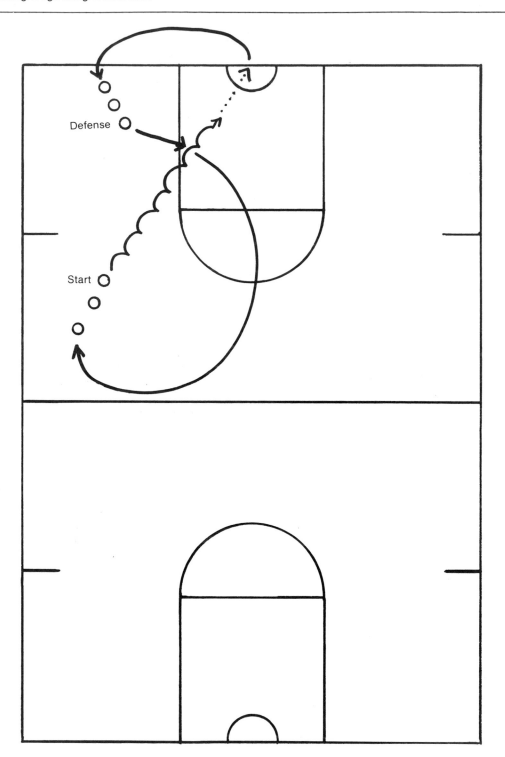

Diagram 6-2. Meanness Drill

The first player drives in for a layup. The defender steps up and fouls him with a push or a hack on the arm as he goes by. This is excellent for learning to get a shot off under control despite physical contact.

Later, move the defenders closer to the basket so they can foul on the shot itself instead of before it.

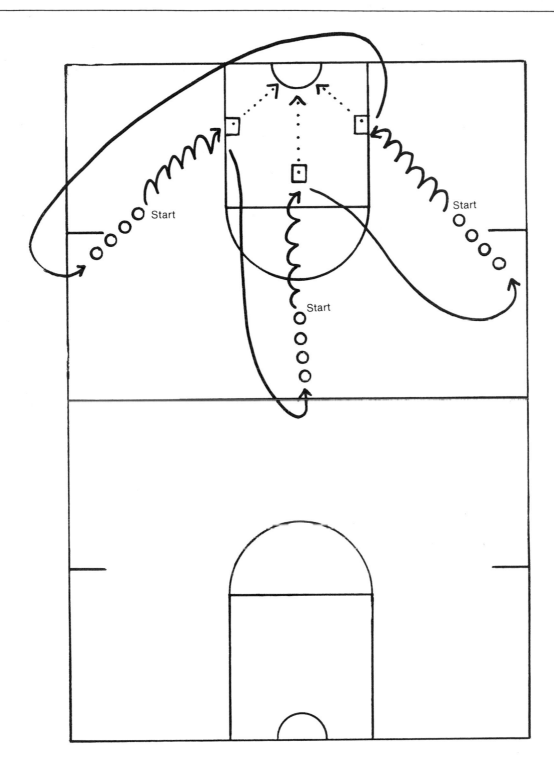

Diagram 6-3. Chair Drill

Start youngsters out on jump shooting with this drill. They must dribble to a chair and shoot the shot. This forces them to go straight up. Make sure they are landing with feet shoulder width apart, providing a more solid base. This will also help when they start rebounding.

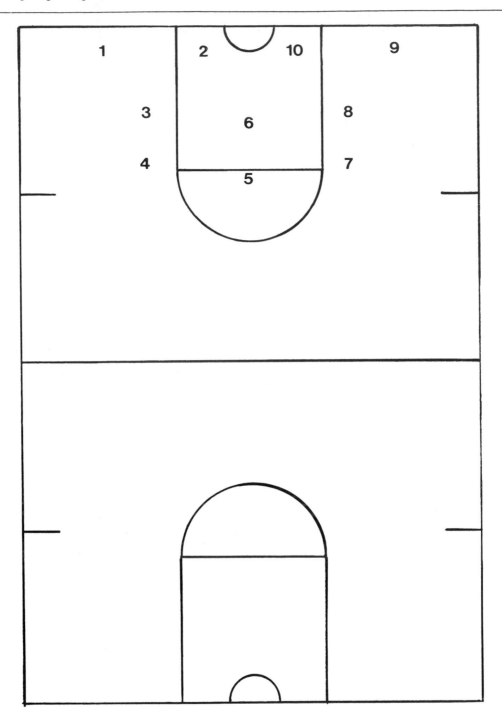

Diagram 6-4. Circuit Drill

Players must shoot ten shots, one from each of the numbered areas, in sequence. The player with highest percentage wins. Shots 2 and 10 are layups. The player must rebound his own shots.

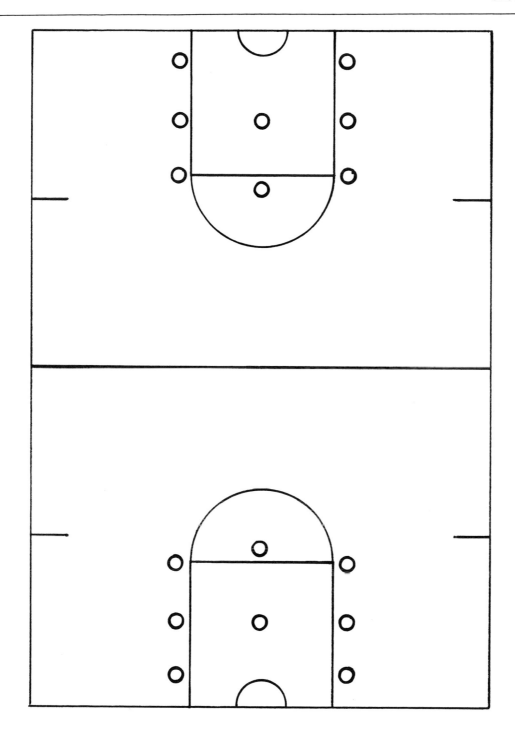

Diagram 6-5. Competitive Shooting

Opposing units station themselves at opposite baskets according to the diagram (if there are fewer or more players, add or delete some positions; put tape on the spots where players will be stationed, if necessary). Each player shoots and rotates to the next position. When all players have shot from all positions, team totals are compared. If time prohibits that many shots each, have each player shoot from one position only, until the shot is made, and keep track of the total attempts.

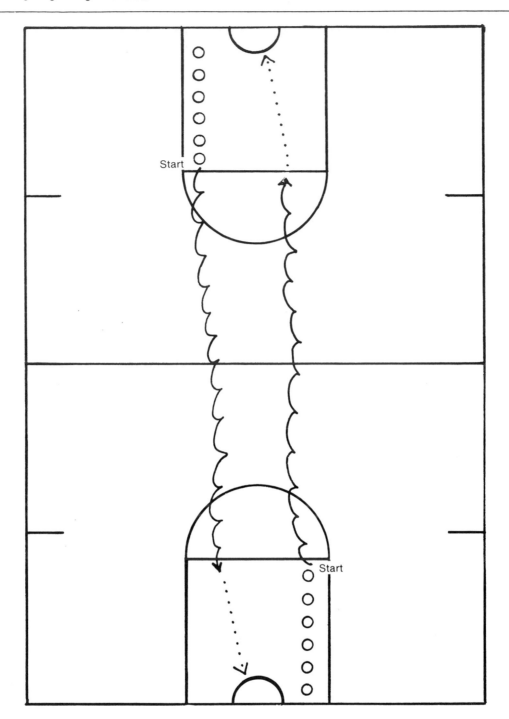

Diagram 6-6. Team Shoot

Each team's shooters must start from the free throw line at one end, dribble to the free throw area at the other end, and shoot. A shooter must rebound his shots and continue shooting until he makes a shot. He then throws an upcourt pass to the next player in line.

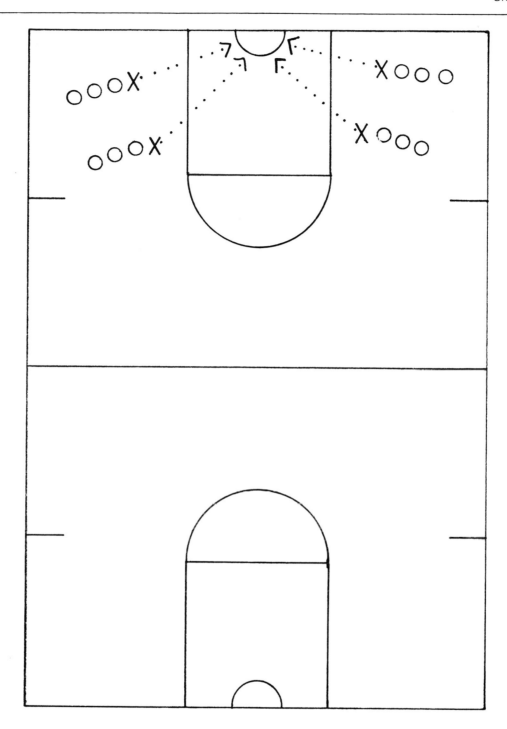

Diagram 6-7. Jumpers

The defenders (X) wave a hand in the face of the shooters but do not block the shot. After attempting the shot, the shooter goes on defense, and the defender goes to the rear of another line.

7

Free Throws

The main ingredients of successful free throw shooting are concentration and relaxation. Most young players are impatient about their shot. They must force themselves to eye the basket before shooting. I suggest selecting the eyelet at the center of the front edge on the rim and looking just past it. If they cannot learn to take enough time, they can count to five first. The player should picture the ball swishing through the net, because the body tends to actualize what the mind suggests.

A consistent routine should be developed. The feet may be shoulder width apart or one foot may be dropped back half a step; but the same stance should be assumed every time. The ball should be bounced with short, hard bounces to help a player loosen up; even the number of bounces should always be the same—counting them may help put the fear of failure out of the mind. The arms may be raised overhead before the shot and the ball taken back to behind the head at the neck as a good loosening-up method. The player should breathe in slowly and deeply, then expel the air (not so much he feels weak or dizzy!) and hold the breath remaining during the actual shot. Breathing in or out during the shot can cause wobbliness.

The player should bend his knees and go upward as he shoots, coordinating the leg movement with the upward arm movement. Some frailer players may have to jump, but if so they must be certain to give themselves enough room so they do not go over the line. If they can always come down on the same spot they began the jump from, fine. Otherwise, more knee flex may add enough power to get the ball to the hoop.

Get players to follow through, again by putting the hand in the basket, as on a jumper.

Free throw shooting (here and on following three pages). Rusty chooses to loosen up prior to his attempt by taking the ball completely back behind his head, stretching out tense arm, neck, and shoulder muscles.

Also get them to follow the shot for a rebound, provided they are not starting forward before the ball reaches the rim.

To help players relax, I tell them just to be sure they hit the rim, preferably the back of it if they are very unsteady. At least then we have a chance to score from the rebound. If a ball misses the rim, it is a turnover even if it does strike against the bankboard. I never tell a young player, "You *have* to make this free throw!" If it is a vital point, he knows it. Adding pressure won't help at all. It is better to remind him that we may still score after a miss as long as he gets the rim. I often just remind him to get enough arch on the ball. Dropping down at a steeper angle increases the chance

that the ball will drop through even if it touches a rim first. A flat shot will bound away.

In games, when another team is at the free throw line, have the player nearest the shooter cut him, i.e., jump directly into the lane in front of him after the shot, preventing him from an easy score should the rebound come directly back toward the free throw line. This is especially important if the shooter puts little arch on the shot, in which case the ball will come back farther.

Don't neglect free throw practice. I have players shoot free throws every day. In any close game, a few free throws make the difference between a win or a loss.

As in a jumpshot, the ball is drawn into the shooting pocket.

The ball is brought upward over the right eye.

The point of release is up over the head.

The shooter follows through with the hand reaching as if being dunked into the basket.

8

Rebounding

Get rebounding position established. The forwards and center should not crowd one another, but should try to slide into a triangular formation (see Diagram 8-2) to cover the greatest area.

Teach players to use their rumps to get more room underneath. Also tell them to back up as far as possible because getting underneath the basket too far will cost them many rebounds. As long as the defender is not allowed to get in front, it does not matter how far back the player is because anything in front of him will be his.

Players must go straight up after the ball. It is hard to resist the impulse to reach over an opponent, especially a shorter one, to grab at the ball, but doing so draws fouls. Tell your players that they must either get a good rebounding position, keeping the opponent behind (called "boxing out"), or else let the rebound go when it comes down to an opponent who got the position first.

Getting a rebound is worth very little if the other team takes it away or our player throws it away. Players must protect the ball. They must take up as much space as possible, get the elbows up and out, and pivot away from the closest defender. The best thing a player can do is outlet quickly. If no outlet is immediately available, the ball should be moved rapidly from side to side. (Here again the elbows are helpful. It isn't dirty to use them if the other team is too pushy about going after a ball that's legally ours; it's a matter of getting some respect from the defenders so they will clear away and allow a pass out to another player.)

A player may take one or two quick dribbles away from the greatest pressure rather than risk getting tied up or throwing the pass away. If possible, a pass should be made immediately, however, particularly if a team is going to fast-

Rebounding. An offensive player is about to shoot over a screen set in front of Number 42.

break. Players in a position to help should do so, calling out to the rebounder to let him know they are there.

Often youngsters will bat at a ball. That's volleyball! Tell them to grab it with two hands and forcibly haul it in.

The worst error of all is failure to jump. Go up hard for that ball! A shorter player can outrebound a nonjumper.

Players don't get rebounds if they aren't there after a shot. Players should talk—"Shot!" when an opponent goes up, "Short!" if his own shot is not long enough and will be coming off the front of the rim, "Long!" if the shot is going too far and can be taken by a teammate on the opposite side of the basket. Players should pivot (remember how important we said those pivots are?) and go in for position *as the shot goes up,* not *after* the shot.

As the shot goes up, Number 50 (lower left) has pivoted quickly toward the basket and is in good position in front of the man he has been guarding (Number 33).

Here 50 has stayed back properly, close to his opponent instead of getting too deep under the basket.

Having kept his opponent squarely behind him with a gliding step, 50 is in excellent position as the ball deflects off the bankboard toward him. Notice that Number 42 has allowed the screener, 23, to hustle around him, but 44 is fighting off his man much better, leaning into him with elbows up and outward.

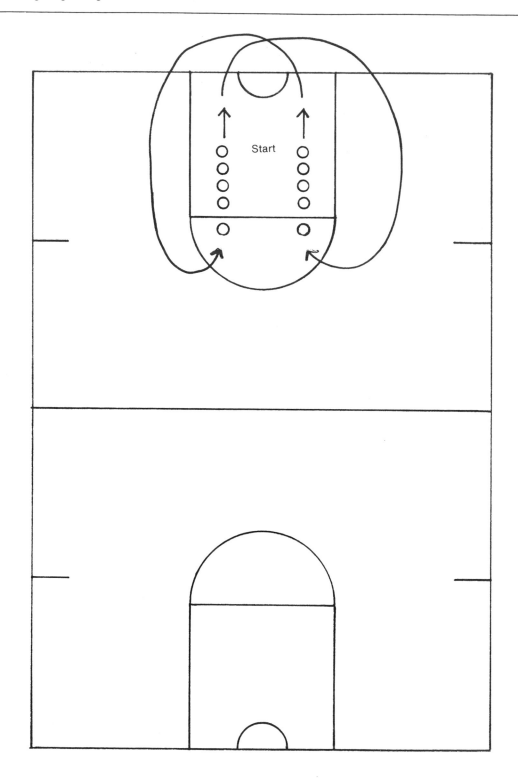

Diagram 8-1.   Two-Line Rebound Drill

Each line tries to keep the ball in the air, with each successive player catching it in the air as it comes off the bankboard and flipping it back, then getting out of the way so the next player can catch and flip it. Good for quickness, jumping, and wrist strength.

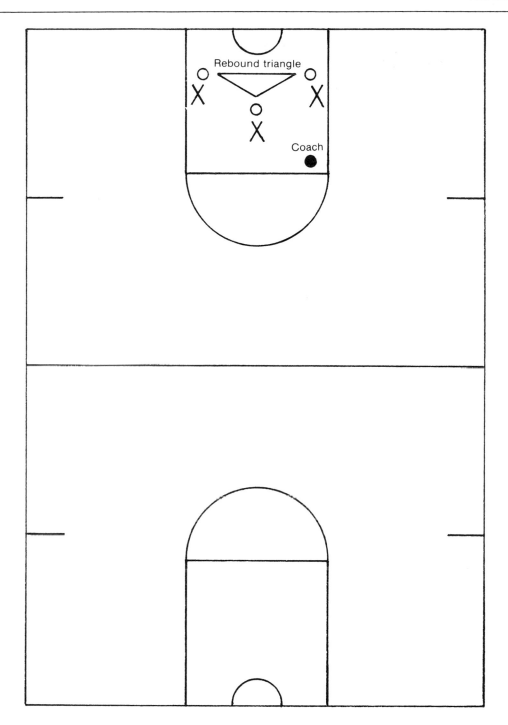

Diagram 8-2. Box-out Drill

The coach shoots and players pivot with the shot, trying to keep the opposing player (X) behind them as they rebound the shot. This is the standard rebounding drill.

9
Basic Defense

Defense is chiefly a matter of positioning. A player should stay between his man and the basket with an eye on both the offensive man and the ball. A player must not overguard the man, because that will allow the opponent to get a step on him and drive around him. In fact, when his man does not have the ball, it is often easier to intercept a pass to him by laying back to lull the passer into thinking the man is open. Then the defender cuts in for the pass, especially if after watching his man he has learned the player does not move toward passes.

In some cases a player may take up a position between the man and the ball, instead of the man and the basket. This is dangerous if the man moves well. The defender must keep track of him by reaching back with a hand to lightly touch him. When he doesn't feel the man there, the player takes a quick visual check and slides back into position again. This practice is called "fronting." It is good to prevent a key player from getting the ball when he has proved to be the other team's best shooter or when the man has too much height advantage to keep him from getting a good shot once he gets the ball. If a man is being doubleteamed, one player can front him while the other takes up the standard defensive position.

Correct the habit many players have of lunging after the ball. They should not take themselves out of defensive position. They must let the offensive man commit himself first to movement in some direction. Lunging also draws too many fouls. It is better to be patient. A good defensive team will maintain position until the offense throws the ball away itself.

When guarding a man well away from the basket, one hand should be low (the hand on the side the ball is on) and one up near the man's face to prevent easy passing.

When a man is playing defense in or near the lane, it is best to keep the hands up high. This makes passing and shooting difficult. If everyone does it, it is the best defense. It is essential, whether the man being guarded has the ball or not.

The athletic stance should be maintained. This is also known as "*getting low*," but I prefer the other term as being more appealing to players. The stance is the same as that used in many other sports—tennis, boxing, baseball, to name a few. It permits quick movement in any direction. The knees are bent, feet shoulder width or slightly more apart, head and back straight and erect to allow a view of the playing area. If players cannot see the value of this position, have them jump from an ordinary standing position, then the athletic stance, to see the difference.

Movement of the feet is in short, quick, sliding steps. The feet should not cross over during lateral movement; in fact, they shouldn't touch.

The steps should come three quarters of the way to the lead foot. I call it *gliding,* not sliding.

If the offensive ball handler is not protecting the ball well, a quick upward slap of the hand may shake it loose without loss of defensive position. Reaching out after it is dangerous.

If a man breaks around a defensive player, he should pivot and quickly race toward the basket, then turn and pick the man up again. It will do no good to run alongside the man— better to outrun him on a direct line to the basket. Also this saves the time wasted looking for where the man is heading.

Guarding the baseline is very crucial to cut down on the other team's scoring. The best way is to line up with the body between the offensive player and the basket, but a step toward the baseline (six to ten inches is plenty). Then the offensive man will have to drive the other way, where the defender is more likely to get help and where getting off a shot is more difficult. If the offensive man does start around, the defender should not trip or use the hands, but slide at an angle to the baseline, brushing the

The defensive player to the left is fronting her taller opponent and, as she watches the ball, is reaching behind to make certain the opponent is still there. The defender in the center is between her girl and the basket, but has an arm in front of her to discourage a pass from Number 42. *Note:* When fronting, a player must not hold her opponent back; if movement is detected, the defender must keep the arms away and block out with the body only.

Number 50 is playing good defense, keeping his weight distributed evenly on the balls of his feet, knees bent, and eyes on the ball handler's midsection.

offensive player with the chest if necessary, instead of sliding directly into him for a foul.

It's up to the coach to get the players to work hard at becoming good defensive players. No youngster finds the job a glamorous one. Yet a team's defense is the most stable element in its playing, and it will win more games than a good offense. There are always one or two games when the offense runs into a slump, and only good defense can save the day. Later we will discuss some motivational methods.

During every pre-season practice, have players go the length of the court one-on-one, the man with the ball switching directions frequently and the defensive man staying in position between him and the basket. This is the basic defensive drill.

In games, whenever a man gets loose with the ball, the defender must call loudly to his teammates, "Help!" or "Switch!" if a teammate's man has blocked the defender from position, in which case the player guarding the man blocking—called *picking*—swaps defensive assignments and shuts off the advancing dribbler.

Here the defender's arms are up because the ball handler is in a high-percentage shooting area, close to the basket. The knees are still flexed, however.

Defensive or athletic stance. The girls bend at the knees and waist but keep the back straight and the head up.

Guarding the baseline. The defensive player has deliberately overshifted toward his left, the baseline side, to stop penetration there. He is taking up as much room as possible to discourage the driver, but is not crowding him.

The dribbler is attempting to drive by on the baseline side, but Number 45 is preventing the move, avoiding a foul call by keeping his hands off and using the chest to stop the drive.

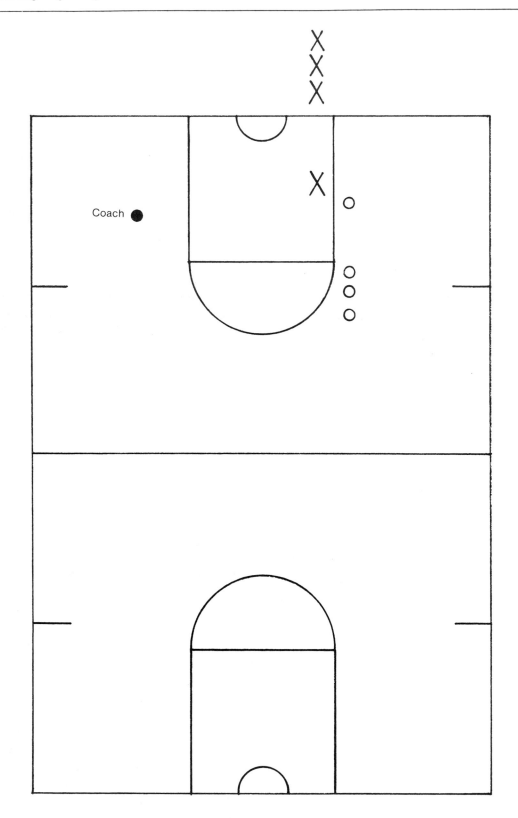

Diagram 9-1.   Prevent-the-Pass Drill

The coach has the ball and O tries to get free from X to
take a pass for a layup.

10

Man-to-Man Defense

Straight man-to-man defense is the most effective in teaching young athletes defensive skills. They develop bad habits if they play zones only, and many high school coaches do not allow junior high assistants to use zones. I employ zones once man-to-man principles have been taught, but some man-to-man defense is used during every game.

Man-to-man play requires quickness and hustling players who recover and regain lost positions. It is the most fun for a fan to watch, since there is more player movement than with the patient zone attacks, during which a team may pass the ball from eight to twenty times before attempting a shot.

The sinking man-to-man is our basic defense. Players move backward into the lane area and do not pick their man up outside. This is effective for us because of a small court. It is not necessary to go too far outside to decrease space

between the defense and opponents, because they do not have much outside room to begin with. It is safer to play near the lane in junior high because fewer junior high opponents are good outside shooters. When we find a player is scoring too much from outside, we let that man guarding him pick him up farther out. Otherwise, we like as many bodies clogging up the lane area as possible. It serves the same purpose as a zone, but does allow easier picks and screens.

PRESS

A press is often effective in junior high because not too many grade school guards can consistently advance the ball against pressure. The full-court press simply means playing man-to-man defense the full length of the court. The biggest flaw in young teams' man-to-man press is that not all of the players react quickly to a change of ball possession. If anyone leaves a man unguarded, the pressuring effect of this defense is lost. When you have a team press, caution them that they are to maintain defensive position but not to start overguarding the man. For some reason, the name "press" seems to bait players into guarding closely and waving arms around, as well as lunging for the ball. This is not necessary and creates fouls.

A half-court press is good for preventing a guard from getting in close enough to start a play. It consists of coming out of the lane area to pick up the man as he comes across the half-court line. Guards will often stop as the pressure arrives and then try to make the first pass of a play from too far away.

In a guard press only the guards play defense the length of the court. This works if you have some bigger, slower players in the game but still have quick ones in the guard position. If the opposing guards do not get their heads up and look for an open pass receiver, this press is just as effective as a full-court press.

It is best to vary the defenses to throw off the offensive tempo. With each change uncertainty and apprehension build up in the opponents as they face a new situation.

Most coaches who use the pressing defenses wait until the second quarter or second half. This avoids early foul trouble and gives the coach a chance to see how quick the opponents are. A quick team or a sharp passing team can rack up quick points against a press. Also, by waiting the players have a look first at their opponents' favorite moves.

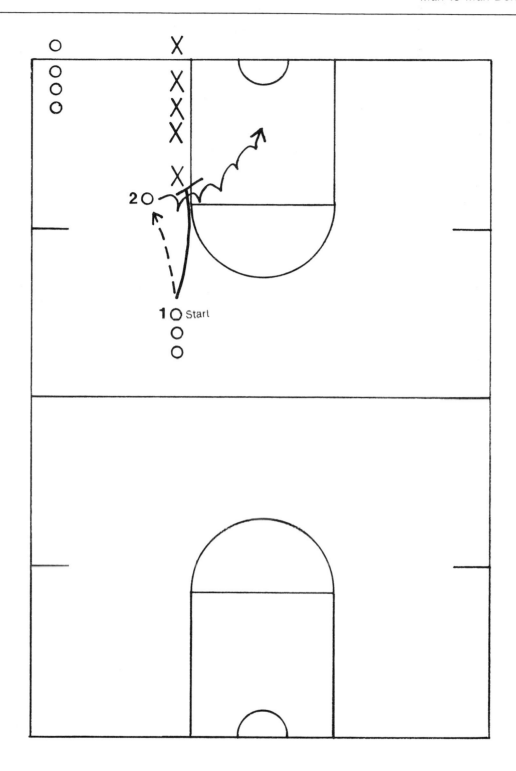

Diagram 10-1. Fight-Through Drill

Here 1 passes to 2 and follows pass to screen off the defender, X. Then 2 takes the pass and tries to use 1's screen. X tries to roll around and through with 2, and if he cannot, he recovers and picks up 2 on the other side of the screen to stop the layup.

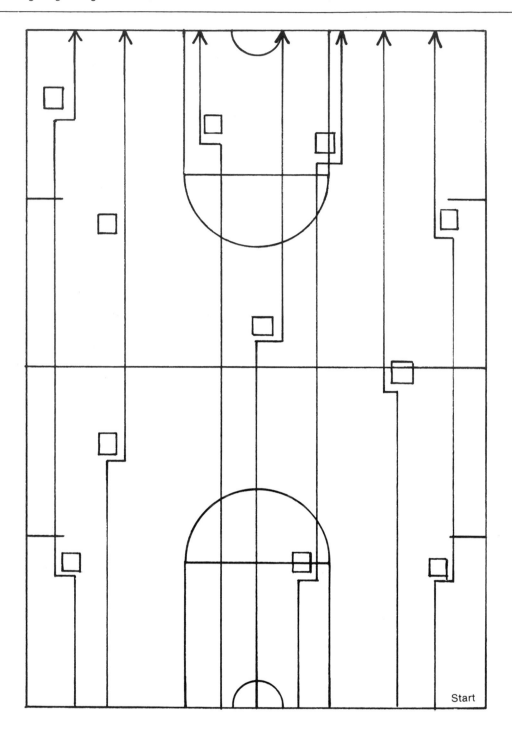

Start

Diagram 10-2.   Find-the-Screen Drill

Players line up at baseline and slide backwards, feeling behind them for chairs placed at random around the floor. They must slide around the chairs and continue backward to the far baseline. Later put an offensive man in each line with a ball and have him try to use these blind picks.

11

Zone Defenses

It is sad that many people consider playing a zone to be nothing more than guarding an area. As a result, players are permitted to stand around nonchalantly until the ball comes into their zone. This is wrong. A zone player is not playing an *area,* he is playing *in* an area and must guard any *man* who enters that area. Thus, he is playing man-to-man within a specific area. He must even be prepared to leave his area momentarily if necessary to pick up a loose ball handler, go after a rebound, grab a loose ball, etc.

Do not use sophisticated, shifting zone defenses on the junior high level. Confusion on the part of the defense presents a scoring opportunity to the offense. We use the following zones:

2-1-2

The most mobile of the taller players takes the central spot and must move with the ball and be prepared to block the progress of anyone who enters the lane. It is best for this player to stay fairly deep because the players on each side of the lane nearest the baseline must go out

farther than the ones playing at the free throw line area to stop shots.

The guards play at the top of the zone and the other two tall men underneath. Diagram 11-1 outlines their area.

2-3 ZONE

This is basically the 2-1-2 with the central man dropped still deeper. It is good against extremely tall teams. See Diagram 11-2.

3-2 ZONE

This allows more coverage against good outside shooting guards. When we play this zone, we no longer have the best tall player in the middle but underneath because there is greater weakness there with this zone.

1-2-2 ZONE

This is much like a 3-2; it is strong against outside shooting and protects the pivot area better than the 3-2. See Diagram 11-4.

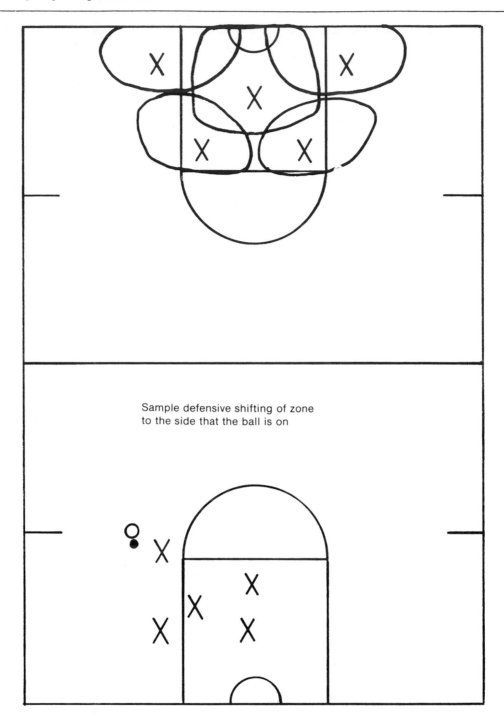

Sample defensive shifting of zone
to the side that the ball is on

**Diagram 11-1.   2-1-2 Zone Coverage
Areas**

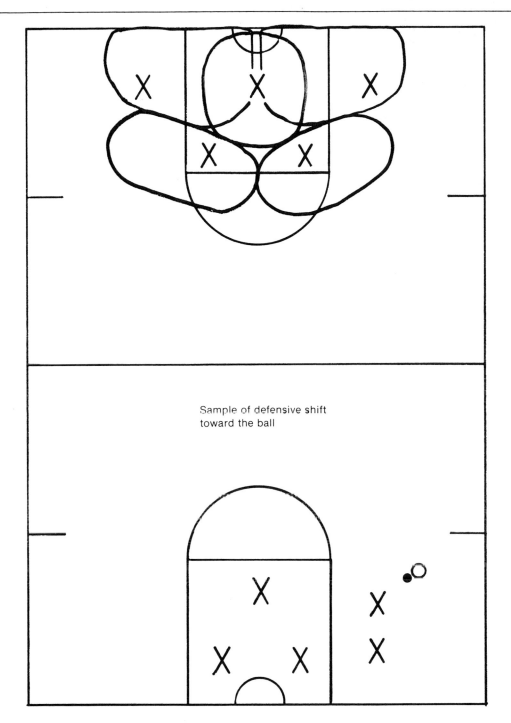

Sample of defensive shift
toward the ball

**Diagram 11-2. 2-3 Zone Defensive
Coverage**

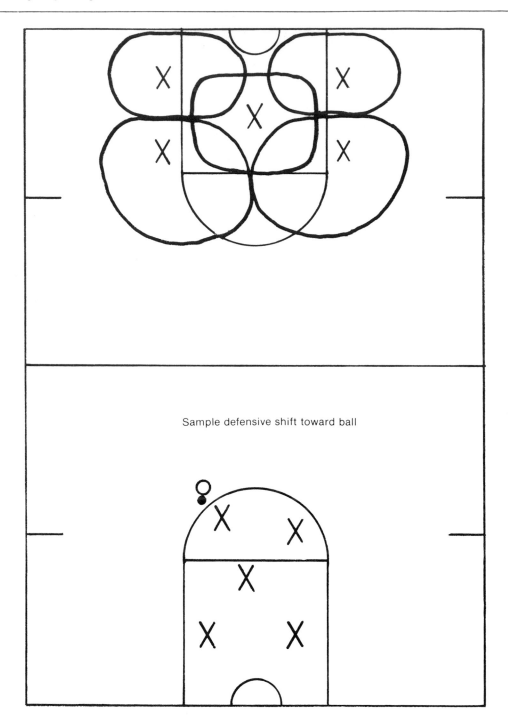

Sample defensive shift toward ball

**Diagram 11-3.   3-2 Zone Defensive
Coverage**

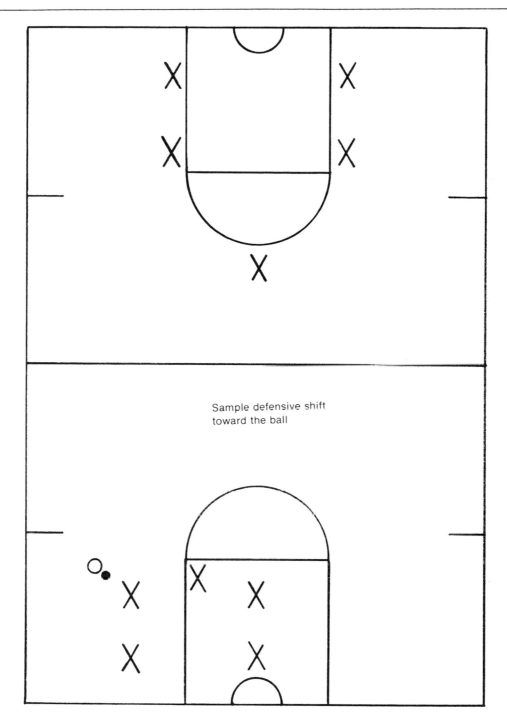

Diagram 11–4. 1–2–2 Zone Defensive Coverage

12

Combination Defenses

Combination defenses are part zone and part man-to-man. The one we use most often is the Diamond-and-One or its first cousin, the Box-and-One. These defenses (Diagram 12–1) keep four players in a zone around the lane area while leaving a rover free to (a) go after the ball, (b) pressure the other team's best player, or (c) sneak upcourt for an easy score after a turn-over. In the first instance (a) we use the guard with the fewest fouls as a chaser; in (b) we use the quickest and best defensive player, and in (c) we use the weaker defensive player of the two guards.

Seldom does a junior high team have more than two really good offensive threats. Therefore, we sometimes go to a triangle-and-two defense (Diagram 12–2) to press these two players and hopefully to keep them from getting a pass at all.

If we are ahead late in the game by a narrow margin and the other team is passing the ball in under their basket, we go to a one-zone in which the best defensive player stays in the lane as added insurance against an easy score off an in-bounds play while the other four go man-to-man, leaving the player passing the ball in loose since he is the least scoring-threat until two passes are made.

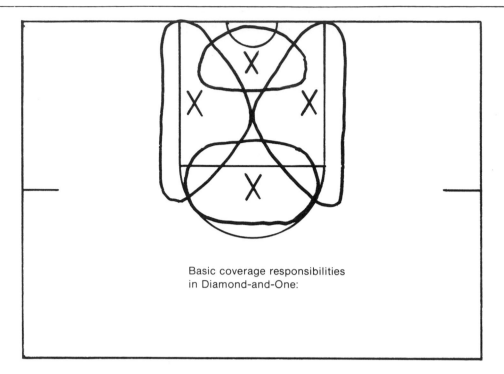

Basic coverage responsibilities
in Diamond-and-One:

Diagram 12-1.   Combination Defenses (1)

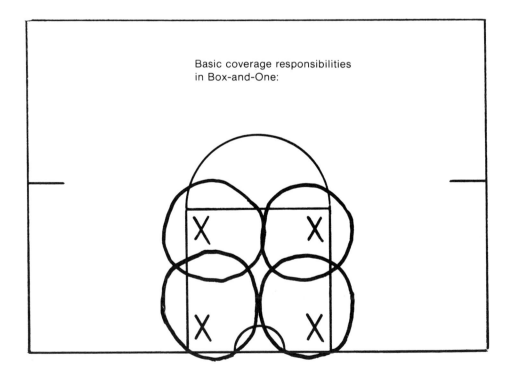

Basic coverage responsibilities
in Box-and-One:

Diagram 12-2.   Combination Defenses (2)

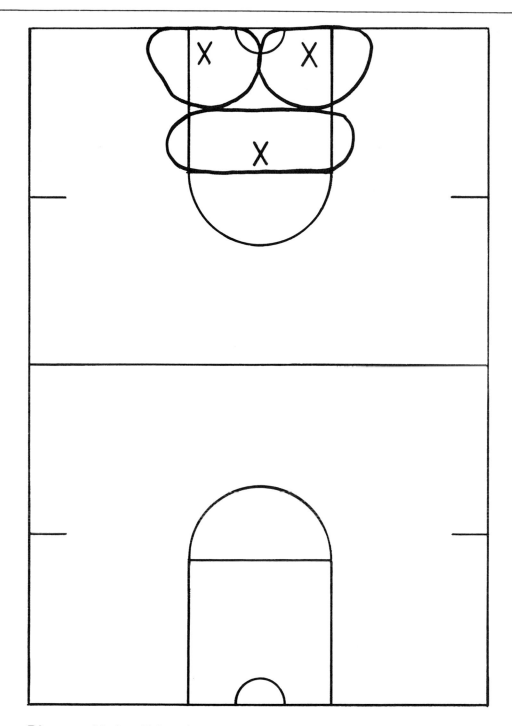

Diagram 12-3. Triangle-and-Two

13

Miscellaneous Drills

The following drills are good for bigger players who need to improve quickness and ball-handling abilities:

SUPERMAN DRILL

The player stands on one side of the lane and shoots off the bankboard so the ball will carom off to the opposite side. He must scramble across to get the rebound. As he comes down with the ball, he fires it across to the other side again and once more hustles after it. He continues until he pulls down the required number of rebounds (usually ten is a real workout), and then after the last rebound he sinks the layup.

REACTION DRILL

The coach holds the ball ten feet behind the player, who is facing away from him. As he releases the ball, the coach blows the whistle. Upon hearing the whistle, the player must pivot and grab the ball. It may be a pass, high or low, or a roll on the floor to left or right, or a lob overhead.

UP-AND-DOWN DRILL

The coach faces the player, who is in the lane ten feet away facing him. The ball is rolled on either side of the player, who bends quickly, grabs it, straightens, and fires it back to the coach, who may move to his left or right. A variation is to have the player grab the ball, pivot, make a layup, take the ball as it comes through the net, pivot again, and fire back to the coach.

Other useful drills are illustrated in Diagrams 13–1 through 13–5.

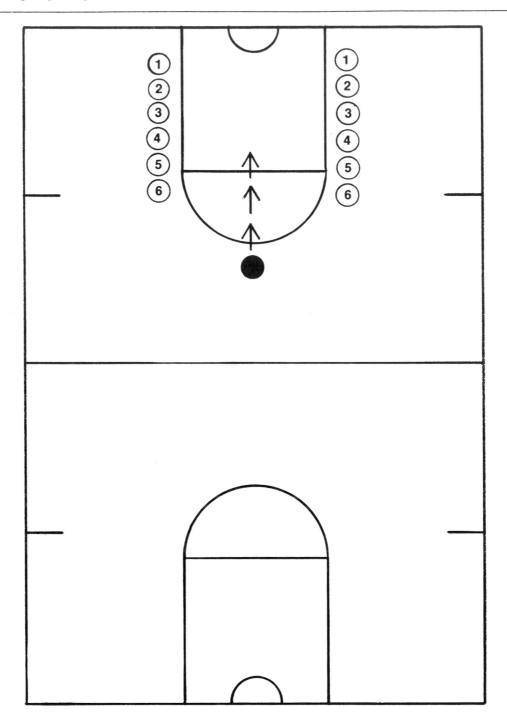

Diagram 13–1.   Steal-the-Bacon Drill

The players pair off, each pair with a different number and on opposite sides of the lane. The ball is rolled down the lane as the coach calls a number. Each player with that number scrambles to get the ball and score. The player who fails to get the ball tries to stop the shooter. A score is worth 2 points for the player's team. If he gets fouled, a point is added whether or not he gets the 2 for a score; if the shot is missed the defensive player's side scores 2.

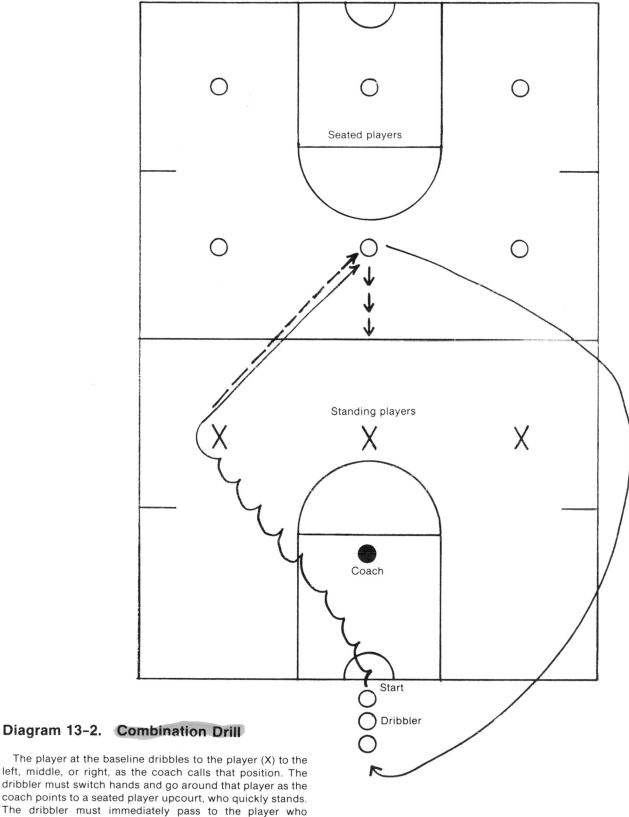

Seated players

Standing players

Coach

Start

Dribbler

Diagram 13-2. Combination Drill

The player at the baseline dribbles to the player (X) to the left, middle, or right, as the coach calls that position. The dribbler must switch hands and go around that player as the coach points to a seated player upcourt, who quickly stands. The dribbler must immediately pass to the player who stands. This forces dribbling with the head up and finding an open man. The receiver passes to the next player at the baseline and goes to that line as the first dribbler takes his place.

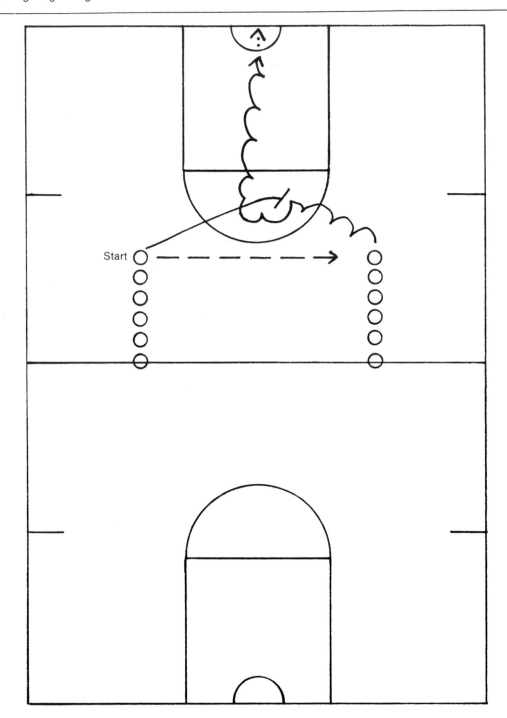

Start

Diagram 13-3. Screening Drill

The player on the left passes to the other line and breaks with his pass to set a screen. The receiver dribbles to the screen, breaks around, and drives in to score. Then he passes back to the first line and goes to the rear of that line while the screener goes to the end of the shooting line.

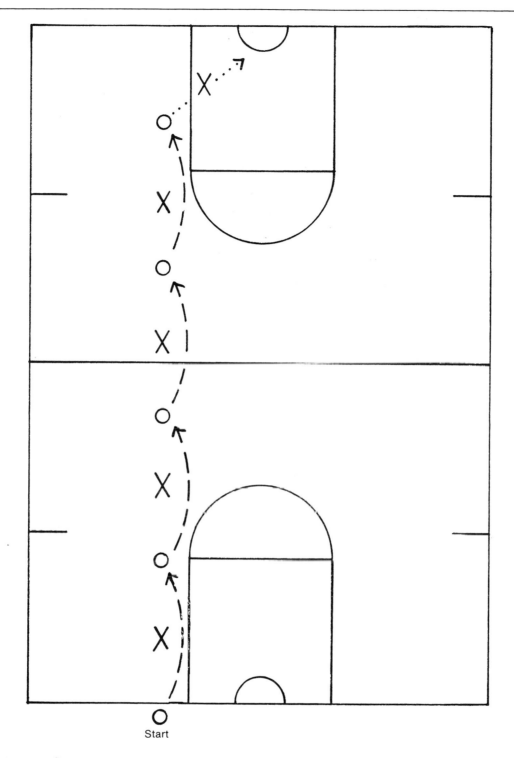

Start

Diagram 13-4. Snake Drill

Opposing players alternate in a line. Starting the ball at one end, one side must try to pass the ball to each succeeding man (overhead or bounce passes) on his side until the last man is reached; this man tries to score over the final defender. The players then rotate one position, with the final defender going to the opposite end to start the passes down the line for his team. The first team to make five shots wins, or best total can win after everyone has shot.

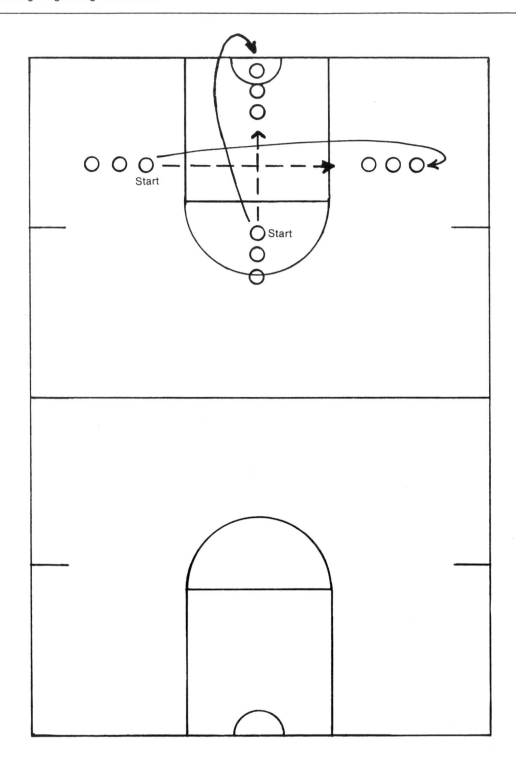

Diagram 13-5.   Two-Ball Crisscross

   This is a sharp-looking, fast-paced passing drill, and it's simple to learn. Players in opposite lines continually rotate, the first player passing and following to the end of the receiver's line. Then that receiver passes and follows across. As one player crosses, the player in the line at right angles to him passes behind him to his own receiving line.

14

Scrimmages

No drill can match a scrimmage for mastering basketball skills. Of course, drills are needed to learn fundamentals and to keep them sharp, but it is in scrimmages that players come the closest to actual game conditions.

Except for the day before a game, scrimmage for at least twenty minutes every practice.

Try to keep units together that will be working together in games. Once in a while it is necessary to put the two tallest players or quickest guards against each other to give them a better workout, but it is good for a unit to learn each other's moves.

It is not necessary to always scrimmage with five on a side. With four or even three on a side, players can duplicate every game situation except actual patterns. Our early-season scrimmages are usually with fewer than five players. For one thing, it is easier to size them up that way.

We have little three-on-three tournaments occasionally to provide a change of pace. Try to balance the teams as much as possible according to height and ability; it can be interesting, though, to pit quickness against height.

We sometimes use a switch-basket scrimmage to quicken defensive reactions and transitions. In this scrimmage a double whistle by the coach signals the offense to change baskets. This means the defense must hustle to get position between the opponent and the other basket.

See Diagram 14-1 for another good scrimmage to sharpen defensive play.

It is a good idea to use the scoreboard for some scrimmages. Set the clock for three, two, or one minute to give players a feel for how much time they have in a game when a few minutes remain on the clock. We also have the score posted so one side may have to overcome a slim lead or hang onto one.

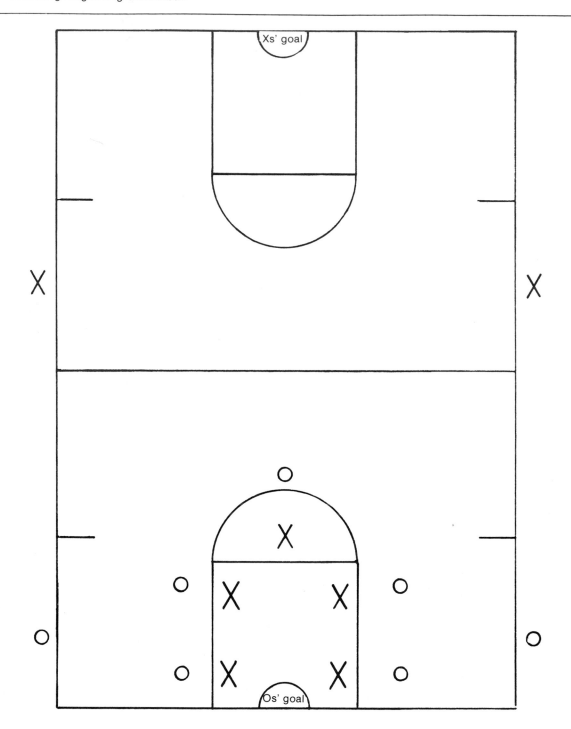

Diagram 14-1.   Seven-Player Scrimmage

When the Xs get a turnover from the offense (Os), they may pass upcourt to one of the players who steps in from the sideline. The two Xs who are assigned as rotators with the players on the sideline must stop at midcourt and go out-of-bounds to a position vacated by the first two, where they are ready the next time the Xs take the ball up. The Os have the same arrangement going the other way.

15

Offense

Teach players to be aggressive on offense. The few offensive fouls they draw will be offset by fouls called against the defense, and aggressive play will mean fewer mistakes, such as loose balls lost and missed rebounds.

The diagrams follow this section for the plays we have used successfully against a man-to-man defense. It is best not to get the offense too complicated. Execution reaps the greatest benefits, rather than complexity. Players who are not sure of their offense will not run it.

If players are not using screens well, I have the screener come to the other player instead of vice versa.

Players can be *keyed* (i.e., signaled for players to begin their movement in unison) in various ways. It is easiest to teach the guard making the first pass to make sure the play has been called, see that the players are set up in offensive formation and then yell "Break!" Another good

way is to key the play to start rolling on the first pass into a forward or the center.

We have names for our plays, as on the diagrams, but they can as easily be numbered or given color names. When we number them, we can agree in a time out to start at a given number and automatically follow through the sequence of plays in order, without their having to be called out by a guard. After the defense has had time to start figuring out what may be coming on a certain number when we have been calling them aloud, we simply agree to add or subtract one or two numbers from the one called to get the number of the actual play. For example, "five" is really Play Number Three if we are going on a minus two; "three" is really Play Number One. Still another way is to call a color and two numbers. If the color is blue it may mean to go by the second number, or on white we may go by the first one. In this way

Pick. The dribbler forces the defensive player (Number 20) backwards into a stationary teammate.

the defense is unable to anticipate a play even though we use just a few plays.

Players must learn to help out another player whose man is giving him trouble, so the teammate will not have to make a blind or wild pass to get rid of the ball.

Players must never turn their backs to the ball. It is embarrassing to have a teammate hit a fellow player on the back of the head with a pass! I've seen it happen many times.

The golden rule of offensive play is to always keep the head up. A player with his head down is all alone on the court.

Liberally praise unselfish teamwork, assists, hustling play, second efforts. Don't dwell too much on who is the high scorer. Give equal time to the rebounding ace, to the guard who controls the tempo for the team, to the player who helps out, or to the sharp passer.

The dribbler now goes around, brushing close by her teammate's shoulder so that the defensive player does not have room to slide by with her.

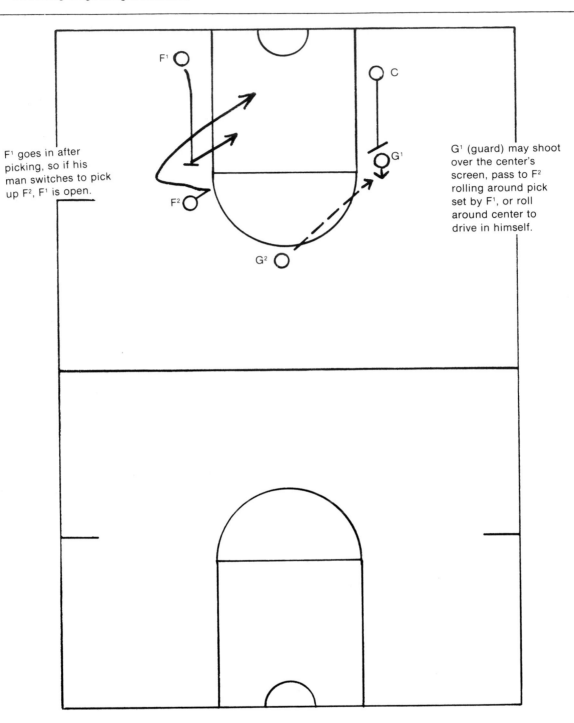

F¹ goes in after picking, so if his man switches to pick up F², F¹ is open.

G¹ (guard) may shoot over the center's screen, pass to F² rolling around pick set by F¹, or roll around center to drive in himself.

Diagram 15-1.   "Gorilla"

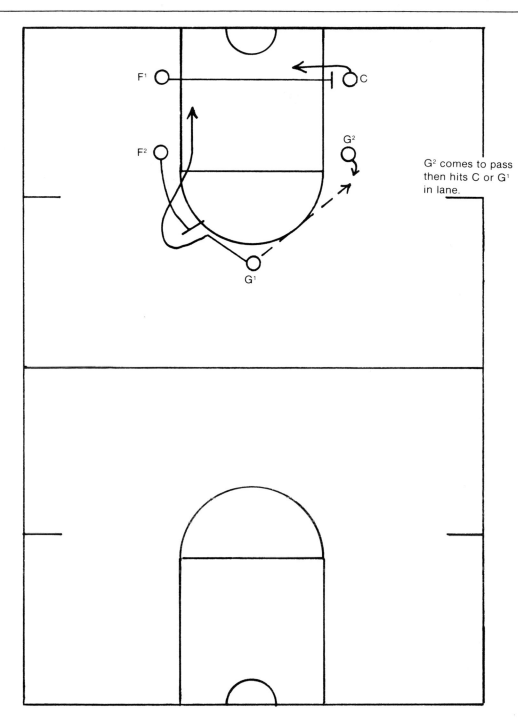

Diagram 15-2. "Scorpion"

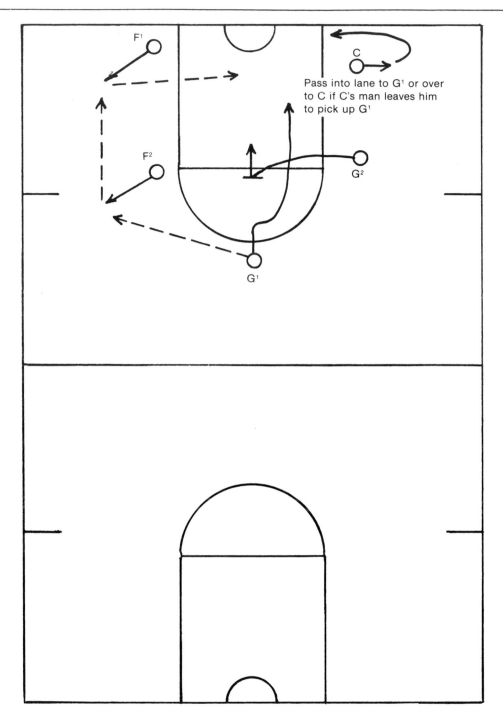

Diagram 15–3.   "Spider"

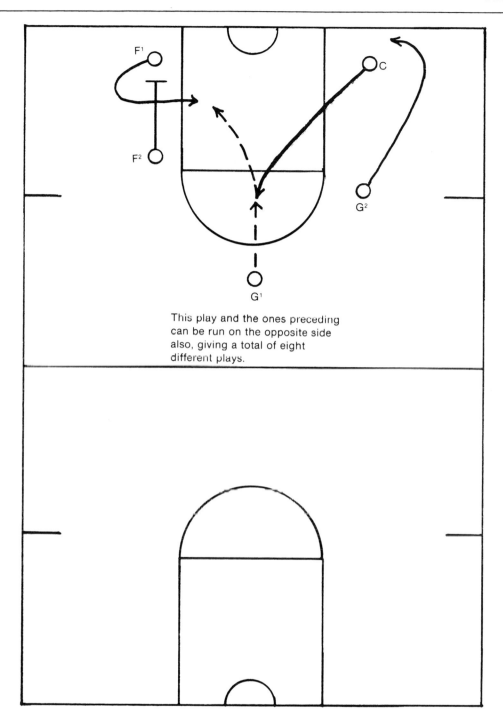

This play and the ones preceding can be run on the opposite side also, giving a total of eight different plays.

Diagram 15-4. "Alligator"

The center takes the pass, pivots, and hits the forward in the lane as he rolls off the other forward's screen. Meanwhile, the other guard is coming around so that if the forward is not open he may have a layup on the other side.

16

Zone Offenses

Use a zone offense against a zone defense.

Players must react quickly when a shot goes up, to rebound and score.

The ball should be moved quickly by crisp passes, to get the defense off balance. When the defense lags behind the offensive passing and someone is left open for a moment, he should take the shot, or if completely open he may take one or two dribbles closer and then shoot. Caution must be exercised to avoid getting bottled up in the lane. It may look open but that won't last long, and hesitation may create a problem.

This offense requires more patience than a man-to-man offense. Prepare your players.

The defense may become impatient and start coming out after the ball. This is when a layup possibility may present itself to an aggressive driver.

The greatest weakness of a zone is that it takes longer to get set up. If possible, the offense should simply beat the defense upcourt and score swiftly before the zone is ready. If this does not happen, players should set up at once in the zone offense and start moving the ball.

Players must not forget to come toward the pass, or the defenders may leap from the zone position to intercept.

The object of zone offensive formations is to get passing triangles set up, so passes can be made with greatest safety into the weak spots in the zone defense.

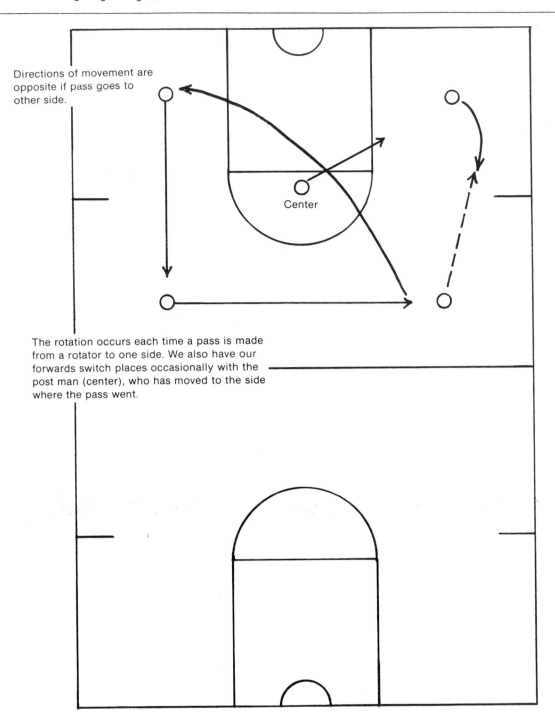

Directions of movement are opposite if pass goes to other side.

Center

The rotation occurs each time a pass is made from a rotator to one side. We also have our forwards switch places occasionally with the post man (center), who has moved to the side where the pass went.

Diagram 16-1.   Rotating 2-1-2 Zone Offense—a Good Offense against the 1-3-1 or 1-2-2 Zone

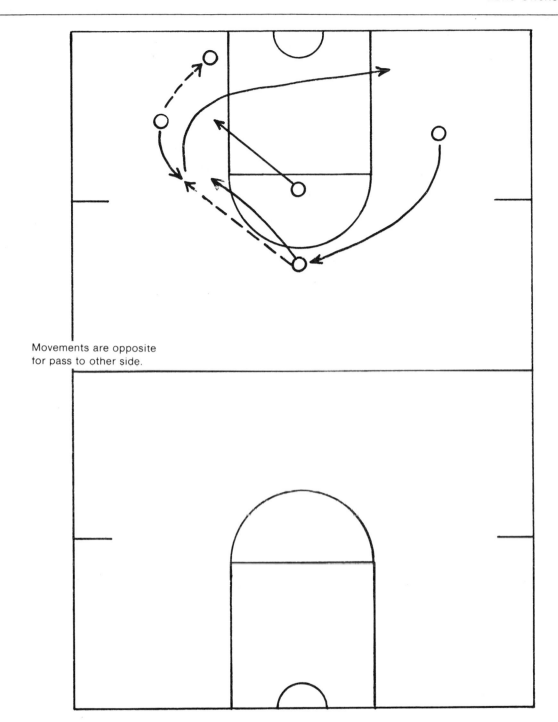

Movements are opposite
for pass to other side.

**Diagram 16-2.   Rotating 1-3-1 Offense—a
Good Offense against a 2-1-2 or a 1-2-2
Zone Defense**

17

The Fast Break

This offense is fun to play and watch. Its quick scoring potential can demoralize opponents. It requires quick thinking to react in time for a fast start; reaction is more important than actual quickness or speed. The most crucial part of the fast break is the first pass from the rebounder to the outlet man; if the passer hesitates, the fast break is gone.

Players must have good heads on their shoulders to keep from throwing the ball away in a helter-skelter rush to score. When the defense gets back to stop the fast break, the offense must have the poise and presence of mind to stop before losing the ball; then the regular offense is set up and run.

In junior high the simplest fast break is the only one that will work, other than upcourt passes to a loose man who has sneaked down for the score earlier (or, if he is not doing his job, who has left the defense on its own and gone on offense earlier than he was supposed to!). We use a sneak play like this from a box-and-one or diamond-and-one defense. Against an extremely weak team it is a cinch score out of a triangle-and-two as well.

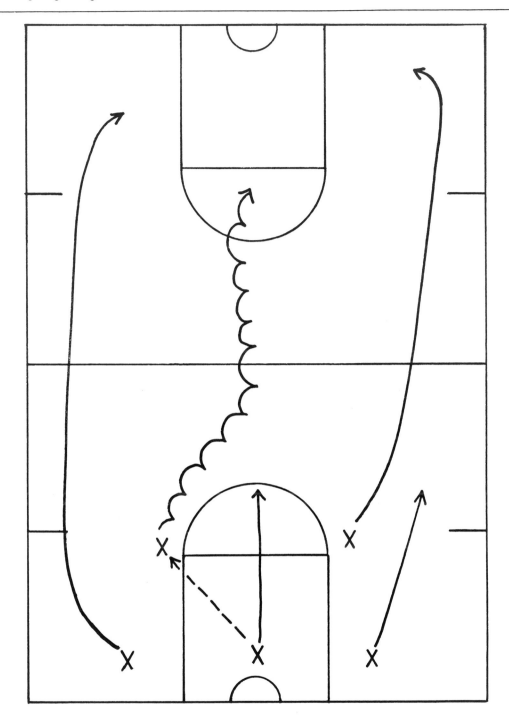

Diagram 17-1. Simplified Fast Break

The rebounder passes the ball to the nearest guard, who takes it up the middle. The rebounder then follows up the middle as a trailer. Whichever guard did not get the outlet pass fills the lane on his side. Forwards who were not rebounders fill their side lanes also. If the center was not the rebounder he fills a side lane. Even simpler is for the center to always be the trailer and the forwards to always fill the side lanes.

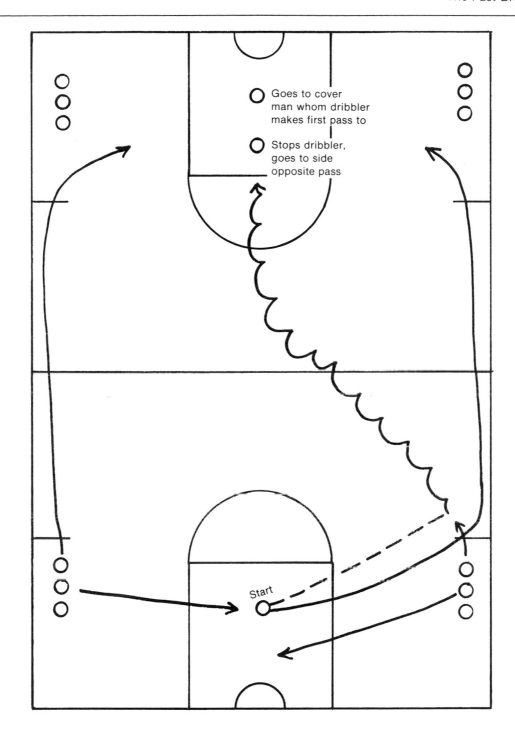

Diagram 17-2. Fast-Break Drill

The man with the ball passes to either side and follows the
pass to fill the lane on that side. The receiver dribbles into
the center, to the free throw line on the far end, where he
passes to either side. The man who was first in line on the
side the pass did not go to at the start has filled the lane on
his side. When the two defenders get a turnover, the drill
continues in the other direction as the rebounder passes
and follows, the receiver takes it to the center, and the other
defender fills the remaining side. Each time the next two
men in line go into the lane to become the next defenders.

18
Breaking the Press

A team that presses you may score quickly and often unless your kids know how to handle it. First of all, it is your role to keep them calm. Let them know that the press simply presents them with an opportunity to score.

We handle the press two ways. The easiest way is to let a good ball-handling guard dribble the ball across the midcourt stripe. This is the best way if the press is a man-to-man press and if the guard is contending with just one other man. Have him wait long enough to let everyone clear away for two reasons: Teammates who remain in the area congest it and keep an extra defender nearby as well; and starting off too soon may leave some defender to the rear, giving that man a chance to come up from behind for a blind steal.

A variation of this simple way to go against a press is merely to change assignments. When we have a taller man who handles the ball well, we use him as our primary target when throwing inbounds. It is also wise to have a taller man throwing the ball in, because he can see over the pressing defense better and get the pass up and over his own defender more easily.

A second way to handle a press, particularly a zone press in which two men come up to put pressure on the guard who has taken the first pass-in, is shown in Diagram 18-1. This is laughably simple, yet it works every time. As soon as there is a basket made or the ball goes out-of-bounds, the players take their positions in a trainlike formation up the center of the court as shown. As the passer-in slaps the ball, the first two men break in opposite directions, with the pass preferably being taken by the second man, who is breaking to the side the pass is coming in from. As the pass goes to this man, the first man in the "train" reverses direction and fills the middle lane. The passer-in rolls around to the outside lane as an extra safety outlet.

Now the first receiver pivots, and as he does the man at midcourt breaks to that side for the second pass. As this receiver pivots, the man upcourt breaks to the same side for the final pass. If this has been handled well, he may either be out front of the defense for an uncontested layup, or he will have a one-on-one situation with the deep man in the zone press, giving him an excellent opportunity to score.

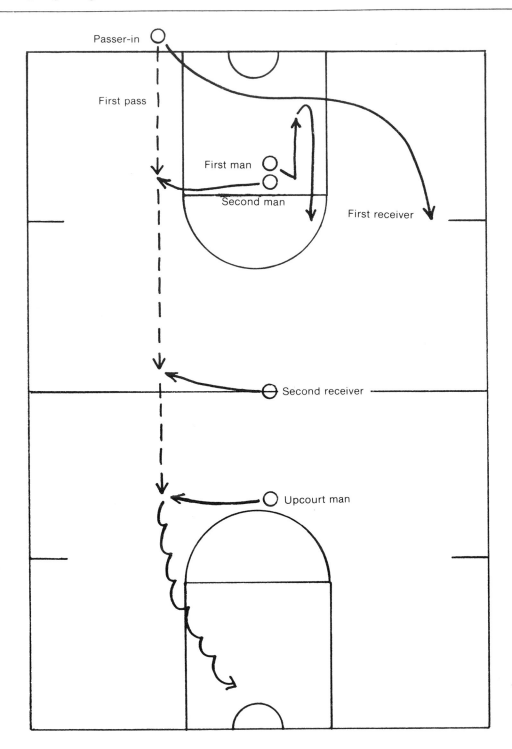

Passer-in

First pass

First man

Second man

First receiver

Second receiver

Upcourt man

Diagram 18–1.   "Train" Pressbreaker

19

Jump Balls

A team can score off jump-ball situations, whether the team's jumper has a height advantage or not. We use the formations in Diagrams 19-1 through 19-3. The first and last are offensive formations, in which we are either sure of getting the tip or at least have a chance equal to that of the other team. The second (19-2) is a defensive formation, in which we are doubtful about getting the tip.

When we are jumping offensively, we like to have a player (a guard if we are away from our basket, a tall man if we are jumping in the circle under our basket) drop back toward our goal and off to one side, where he has a chance to drive in for the quick score on either a direct tip from our jumper or on a quick relay from another player to whom the ball is tipped. We have our jumper look around the circle just before the jump, and he is directed to go to the safest side of the most open man. The safest side is the side of the man away from his nearest opponent. We always have one player on the other team's basket side, just in case the jump is

mistimed or the other team gets the ball by cutting in front of an intended receiver. We don't like it when this happens, because we feel *we* should do the moving in after the ball, not them, but it does sometimes occur.

An important point to tell your youngsters is that they can legally move into the circle as the ball is tipped; they do not have to wait outside until it comes to them. In fact, until a referee calls us for moving in too soon, we try to make a move for the ball as it is still going up for the tip. The only danger with this, ordinarily, is that the jumper can bat the ball over the head of his receiver. He should not bat it hard (unless going to the deep man), but *tip* it.

When we jump defensively, the three players at the circle are all instructed to watch the direction the opposing jumper's palm is facing, or which way his eyes go just before the tip is up. Thus trying to anticipate what his target will be, we can often intercept even though the opponent has outjumped our man, as we cut in front of the intended target.

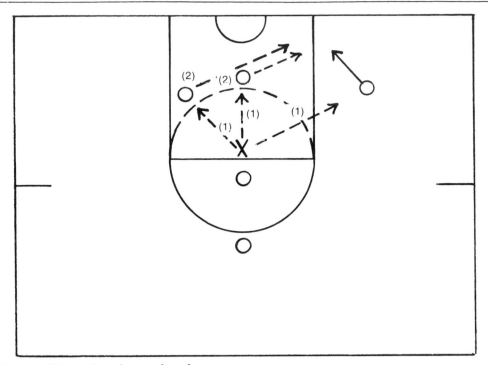

Diagram 19-1. Offensive Jump (under our basket)

The jumper may hit any open man, preferably one of the three on the side of our basket. If the deep man is not the receiver, the pass should immediately go to him as he cuts quickly in for a layup.

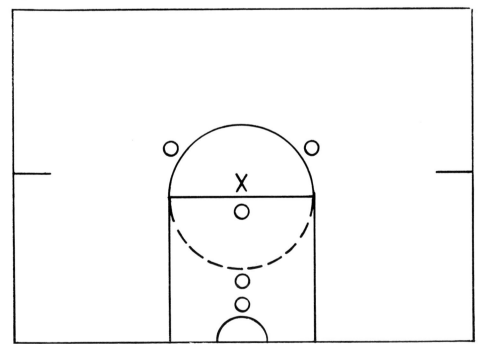

Diagram 19-2. Defensive Jump

The safety man, under their basket, must not commit himself until a drive for the shot is actually being made, because the opponent taking the tip may pass over him to the opposite side of the lane if he moves too soon.

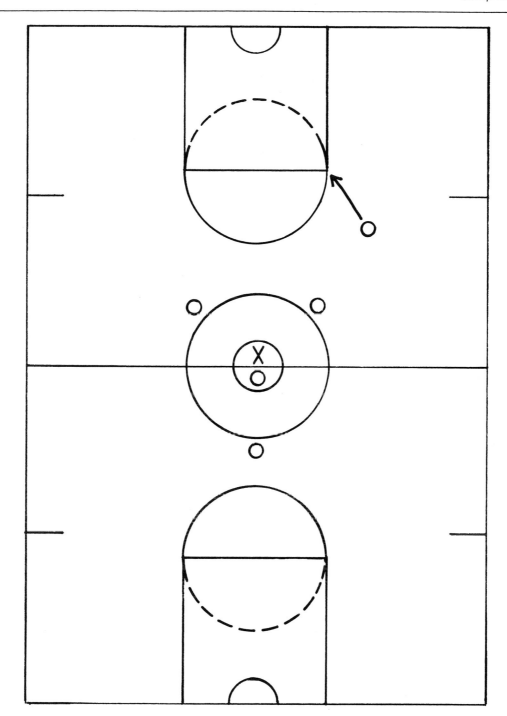

Diagram 19-3. Offensive Jump (away from our basket)

If possible, the deep man sneaks deeper still for a free basket. He is away from the circle and less likely to be called for movement. He should not turn his back to the jumper as he moves, because the attempt may be made to him. Since he may be moving toward the goal, the jumper should tap the ball on the basket side of the deep man if he goes to him, or it may go out of bounds behind the man.

20

Inbounds Plays

Inbounds plays are used when a team is passing the ball in under their own basket. Two or three such plays are enough in junior high school. The man passing the ball in should call the number of the inbounds play loudly, and more than once, before the referee ever hands him the ball. The other players will then have time to scramble into position and to think about the move they are to make when the ball is slapped to key the play.

When the ball is passed in from out-of-bounds areas away from the basket, we do not use these plays but simply have all players find a spot on the floor well away from any teammate, giving them more room to work free. Then they should get open, not by running away from the defender, as most try to do, but by first moving *into* the defender, then leaping away.

Diagram 20-1 shows the play we use under our basket when we have a player with a definite height or jumping advantage over any player on the other team. If this is the case, we may use this play almost every time, because it is impossible to defend against if worked correctly.

If we have no great height advantage, we still slip in the first play two or three times during a game, because it will often work if the opponents are not expecting it; they are looking for a move first, probably into the lane, and this gives the edge to our receiver, who knows where the pass is coming.

All these plays are run on either side of the basket, using the same number but actually mirroring the plays as shown when run on the other side.

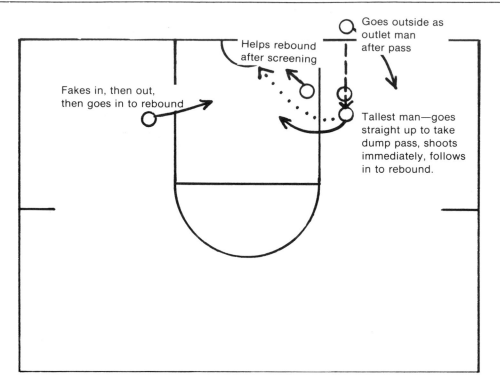

Goes outside as outlet man after pass

Helps rebound after screening

Fakes in, then out, then goes in to rebound

Tallest man—goes straight up to take dump pass, shoots immediately, follows in to rebound.

Diagram 20-1.   Inbounds Play (1)

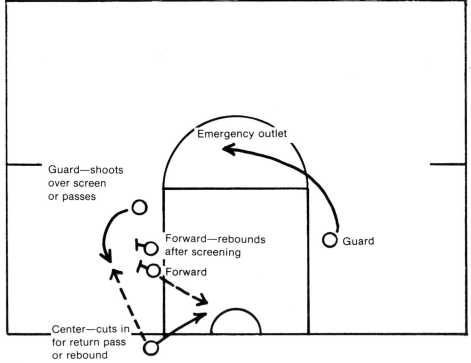

Emergency outlet

Guard—shoots over screen or passes

Forward—rebounds after screening

Forward

Guard

Center—cuts in for return pass or rebound

Diagram 20-2.   Inbounds Play (2)

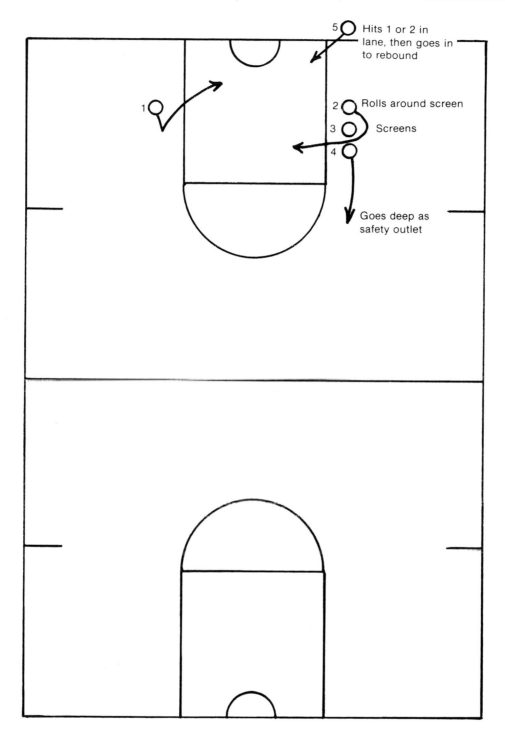

Diagram 20-3.   Inbounds Play (3)

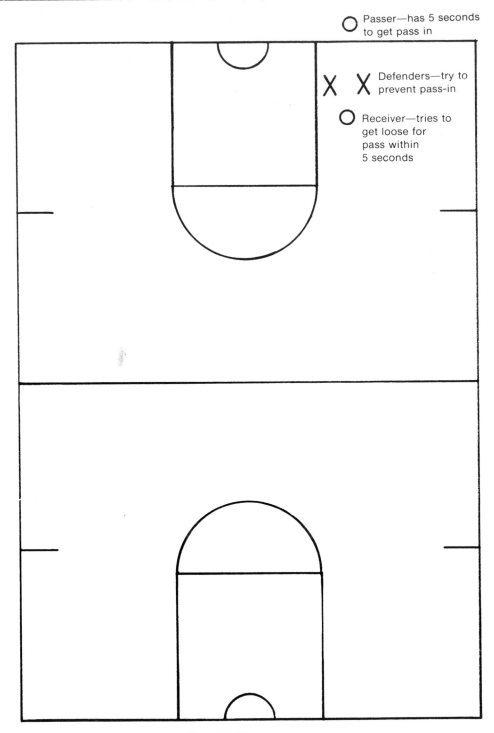

Diagram 20-4.   Inbounding Drill

21

Stall or Delay

Many coaches frown on the use of stalling tactics, especially on the junior high school level, for three reasons. First, what got the team ahead should keep them ahead. Second, if the margin is narrow, hanging onto the ball may result in a costly turnover when the team might otherwise have increased the slim lead. And third, taking time to teach a stall or delay means less time spent on more important fundamentals. In addition, some spectators think the stall game is boring or even unsportsmanlike.

On the other hand, the team that has a lead and stalls is more likely to draw a foul from the opponents. If the team's free-throw shooting percentage is low, this could, of course, be impractical. But if a team has some good ball handlers, percentages say the stall or delay pays off more than a normal offensive attack late in the game. Personally, I think the stall can be exciting, and as long as the object of the game is to win, it will be used by most coaches. However, because I don't think it is worth spending too much of a young player's practice time in learning it, we do not use a complex stall or delay pattern.

What we try to do when ahead late in the game is to slow the pace down without undue passing and dribbling. This means we hold the ball until pressure starts coming up, then pass it. We stay well outside our usual offensive positions, where we have more room. We try to help out with zigzags and cuts and to get the ball as often as possible to the best ball handler. Finally, we take no shot except a layup.

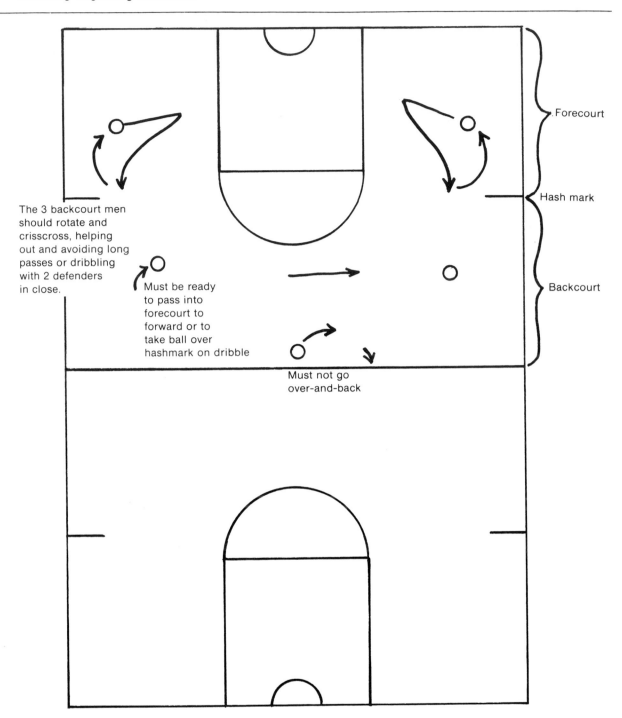

The 3 backcourt men should rotate and crisscross, helping out and avoiding long passes or dribbling with 2 defenders in close.

Must be ready to pass into forecourt to forward or to take ball over hashmark on dribble

Must not go over-and-back

.Forecourt

Hash mark

Backcourt

Diagram 21-1.   Slowdown Offensive Formation

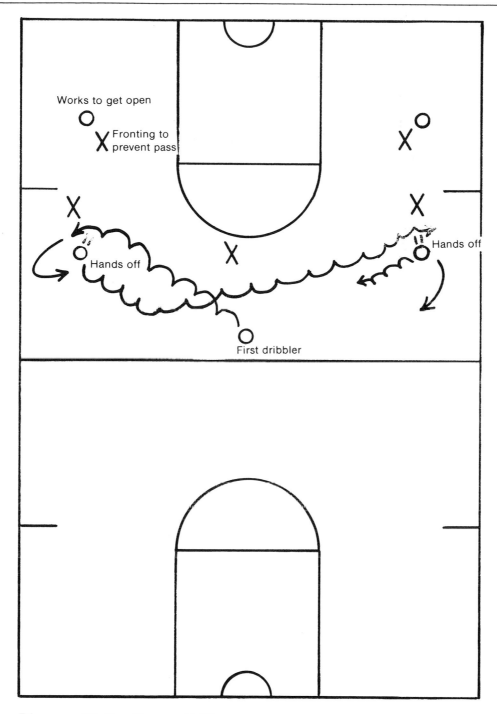

Diagram 21-2. Freeze Drill

22

Pregame Warmups

It is hard for young athletes to play a good first quarter when they are not loosened up or when they look and feel like scrubs before the game begins. Sharp, organized pregame warmups circumvent these handicaps, and are pleasing to watch as the crowd awaits the game action.

We do not have time to spend developing a separate pregame warmup routine, so we simply use some of the standard drills we have used as part of regular practice sessions. The team captain is in charge out on the floor, telling the others when to start the next exercise.

I tell the kids to look like pros even when they goof. It is one thing to lose control of a ball, and quite another to make a big thing of it with overreacting. A player who knows he is good will shrug off a mistake and keep going.

Some of the drills I suggest for use before games are illustrated in Diagrams 2-2 (run the weave from halfcourt), 3-1, 5-5, 5-6, 6-1, 6-7 (looks much more organized than general shooting as a warmup), 13-3, and 13-5. Diagram 8-1 is good if the kids can handle it well; you may want just the first five or six players to do this while the others form circles and pass the ball around.

Shooting a few free throws is also a good idea. Make sure the kids take this seriously and do not clown around while waiting at the rebound line.

23

Motivation and Sportsmanship

The first job you have in terms of motivation is to be the kind of person for whom kids want to work. If you do not love kids, you are in the wrong field. Not only should you love them with all your heart, you should also let them know it, and then prove it by your actions. Know them as individuals. Praise them when they do better than usual. When they know you truly care, you can be a firm disciplinarian, and they will accept it from you. Otherwise, they will very justifiably rebel.

Before the season ever starts, get to work! Get the potential players revved up. Talk basketball to them. Ask them if they're practicing by the garage. If possible, open up the gym for them during the off-season. I open our gym on Saturday mornings during the season as well; it increases our shooting percentage. Put up signs around the school announcing practices coming up. Place an announcement in the local paper.

Recruit. That's right—even in junior high school, you must be a recruiter. The people you are recruiting are the ones who would otherwise sit in study hall during the season, when physically they have great promise as athletes. Many assume they are no good because they haven't played before. Nonsense! In junior high school, it's not too late to begin. Tell them to give it a try. What can they lose? If they don't try, they won't be playing in high school, for sure, and they may always wonder if they could have made a team. One of the three best players I have ever had never played basketball until forcibly dragged from a study hall by yours truly. That bit of recruiting made a worthwhile difference in the player's life and helped the team to several victories we would have certainly not gained otherwise.

At the start of the practice season, put up a bulletin board. Include such things as pictures from magazines of ballplayers; great stars' tips on shooting; clippings from previous years' newspaper coverage; the season's playing schedule; charts of performance ready to be filled in (we keep a free-throw percentage chart from practices and a game performance chart on which a player earns a star of a certain color for over ten rebounds, over eight points, best defense played, and four or more assists); and slogans like "When the Going Gets Tough, the Tough Get Going."

After every game, send an article to the local paper. In smaller towns, these are usually welcomed. You may even be able to contact a radio or television station if the season is going particularly well. In the publicity I send out, I try to get in as many players' names as possible, especially if they do not often get recognition.

Talk to individuals and to the team about how good they can be. Convince them, and they will be great.

Make up a manual of team records, rules, schedule, fundamental tips (feel free to use the ones from this manual), and plays. It makes kids feel "pro" to have such a manual issued to them. Just mimeograph it off, draw a cover for it, and staple it together. Warn them to hang onto it and to never let anyone but a parent or teammate see it.

Get your spouse to come to some games with a camera. Put some photos of the players in action on the bulletin board, and send some to the newspaper with your articles.

Let them know there will be some special award, such as a performance certificate or free pizza at a team party after the season, for the most improved player, the most inspirational, etc.

On the bus going to games, don't let them get too silly. They should prepare themselves mentally for a contest, going over their plays, etc.

Distribute information to them about summer clinics available. These clinics dramatically improve a young person's playing level. Encourage them. If they want to be the best,

they'll have to pay the price.

If possible, set up a little summer intramural league, perhaps three-on-three teams. Have a responsible young person arrange the matchups, or teams can get together each week with the team they are scheduled to play that week to work out a time. Publish results at the end of the summer.

At the end of the season, distribute a handout of drills they can use during the summer. Not many will follow them, but if even one does (and more than that probably will), it will help the next year's team get off to a headstart. Use some of the ball-handling drills and shooting drills illustrated in this manual.

Don't make a bunch of rules for the team when the season begins, or you may get yourself into a predicament. Players know they shouldn't do certain things. Deal with each situation on an individual basis, but be fair. Don't kick a reserve off the squad for something a starter could get by with.

Check with other teachers on the players' grades. It is better to chat with them about getting their grades up *before* they are flunking and have become ineligible.

Build a tradition. Let the kids know they are winners, in life as well as sports. Tell them they are fine young people, and that they are good sports. If a player on another team wants to get rowdy or obnoxious, that is simply an opportunity for your players to show they are above such things. If fans in opposing towns have some disparaging comments, your players should totally ignore it. Games are won on the court, and mouthiness doesn't alter the final score.

Appearance is important. People act the way they look. Have the kids spruce up a little on game days. I even insist they wear tennis shoes and socks of the same color in games. If your team's uniforms aren't the best, badger the town's booster club or the school board to get them into something that looks sharp.

24

Miscellaneous

KEEP RECORDS

Keep track of what teams you play, the scores, and individual players' performances. After the season I distribute a handout of statistics—free-throw percentages, field-goal percentages, rebound totals, etc.

SCOREBOOKS

Get an understandable scorebook from your local sporting goods store, and find the most reliable student you can to keep score during games. Save the scorebook from each season because it may help you prepare for games later. Also, make a note on each page of the scorebook about what type of defense the team played; make sure you get their coach's name, too, because a new coach the next year may use a different defense (so might the old coach, but this isn't as likely).

CHARTS

Don't keep complicated charts. The ones I like to use are diagramed (24-1 and 24-2).

STUDENT MANAGERS

Find some good student managers (two or three), and give them recognition along with the players. Make certain they get a list of exactly what you expect from them. Duties include pumping up balls, getting balls into the locker room before games and at halftime for the captains to lead the team out with, scrubbing the locker room floor twice a week with antiseptic detergent to prevent foot diseases, keeping free-throw charts up-to-date, packing the medical kit, getting all supplies onto the bus for road trips, keeping players' valuables in a bag where they won't be lost or taken, bringing the scorebook in to you at halftime so you can check for players in foul trouble and the other team's high scorers, getting the scoreboard turned on for practices, clearing the gym floor of any obstacles, checking the locker room after practice to make sure showers and lights are out and no articles of clothing are left behind, bringing you your whistle or clipboard when you need it, taping up weak ankles or knees, bandaging minor scrapes and cuts, and staying near you but out of the way during games and practices in case they are needed.

CUTTING

It is best to avoid cutting in junior high because young people may change so considerably in a short time that a potentially good athletic career may be destroyed by the practice of cutting. If the facilities and the number of candidates forces you to cut, make certain you explain your decisions will be based strictly on player's ability to help the team, not on any likes or dislikes of yours. Failure to do this may seriously wound a youngster. If very many must be cut, you might set up an intramurals league for them, perhaps with the incentive that you will suit up the week's top performer or two for the next week's games.

TIME OUTS

Take a time out when there is a scoring surge by the other team. Don't unsettle your players further by acting upset yourself; instead, be very self-assured and mechanical in the huddle. Don't take a time out when your players have momentum going their way. If there is an injury, the time out is charged to you only if you leave the injured player in the game after attending to him, so it is usually best to send in a substitute. Take a time out to set up an important play near the end of a close game, if necessary. Near the end of the fourth quarter, the other coach will probably take a time out if the score is close but in your favor. When he does, tell your players to avoid fouling since it is advantageous to them to keep the clock going. If the situation is reversed, you will have to call a time out and tell your players not to panic. When they have more than a two-point deficit

in the score with under twenty seconds remaining, or one to two points with ten seconds, have the player nearest the first opponent to get the ball, foul him. (Have him foul by going aggressively after the ball, not making it look deliberate, if possible; a deliberate foul is two shots instead of a one-and-one.) If it is late in the game and they have a player at the line to shoot a crucial free throw, it is wise to call a time out to give the shooter more time to get nervous about the shot. I also call time outs when I want to change the offense or defense. If I want to have a switch in guarding assignments, I send in a substitute with that information. If there is confusion on the part of some player about what defense or offense we are using, or if an opposing player is being left unguarded, I call a time out to correct this before it costs us points.

HALFTIME

At halftime, if you are behind, get the players to fire up more by letting them know you think they can do much better. Stress going after loose balls and being more aggressive overall. I tell them I'll give anyone who fouls out a candy bar, if it seems they are playing in too timid a manner! Also halftime is the time to set up the next quarter's offensive or defensive changes, to switch some players' assignments if the coverage could be better, to arrange to shut off some particularly effective opponent, and to correct individual errors—failure to protect rebounds or outlet quickly, sluggishness in making the transition from offense to defense, running an offensive pattern incorrectly, leaving the baseline open, failure to get the arms up in the lane, lunging too much, etc. Don't lose your cool and swear or let them think you're enraged with them. This will only shake them up more or even make them transfer their frustration to you. Appeal more to their pride and self-respect. Let them know the game is not over after only two quarters. Remember—it's *their* game, *their* sport, and you can't force them to win if they don't want to badly enough! Your job is simply to tell them what they must do to win; then it's up to them. I've tried all the other ways, and I found it is best to keep my head.

SUPPLIES

For trips, make sure you have the medical kit, enough basketballs, the game charts and scorebook, chalk and a small chalkboard if available, uniforms, extra support straps for glasses, shoestrings, and all your players!

TALKING TO OTHER COACHES

When other coaches tell you they are losing games, their best player is sick or declared ineligible, etc., take it with a grain of salt. Once I believed such a line so completely that I started my second string. We fell eight points behind in the first two minutes. When the starters went in, they had a struggle to catch up, finally winning in overtime. Don't tell other coaches you're going to beat them. Any junior high team can hit a bad day and lose to any other team. Be friendly, but not too informative. Don't reveal your game plan—be vague.

INJURIES

It is possible to prevent most injuries. Wearing two pairs of socks eliminates most blisters. Having your players in condition will keep them from getting hurt most of the time. Don't fall apart if a player gets a bump or scrape, or the others will often get paranoid about minor things. For jammed fingers, tape the jammed one to the next finger or the fingers on each side. You can't let players have popsicle sticks to support a finger in a game (incidentally, make sure they aren't wearing jewelry in games or practices, either). Only rest seems to do much for shin splints. Knee injuries and possible fractures of arms, wrists, or elbows are best taken to a doctor. Don't risk a young person's health and well-being by playing him with a potentially serious injury. Prescribe heating ointment such as Icy Hot or Ben Gay for muscle aches. Put ice on nastier bumps or twisted ankles, and keep ankles taped for a week or two after a twist, since the first twist weakens them and can lead to a more serious one. Have a manager massage hurting leg muscles or aching (but not injured) backs. Put pads in the shoe for bruised heels.

If an injury is extremely grave, keep the youngster warm and motionless and keep talking gently and reassuringly to him to avoid shock. Get him some medical attention quickly. If a limb is broken, don't mess around with it—get a flat piece of wood and lots of padding under it, and move him with extreme caution.

ETIQUETTE

Meet the referees before the game. Treat them like human beings during the game. No matter how it looks to a losing side, no referee is trying to cheat; if the calls are bad ones, chances are the calls are bad for both teams. After the game, thank the referees for their job if it wasn't obviously inferior. Shake the hand of the opposing coach before and after the game. Mention any of his players whom you noticed played exceptionally well.

Opponent _____ Date _____		
Name & Number of Player	Shots	Free Throws
	2.00 2.2.000 O = missed shot 2 = shot made	○ ● ● ○ ○ missed free throw ● made free throw

Diagram 24–1.   Shot Chart

Opponent _____ Date_____					
Name and Number	Rebounds Offense	Defense	Turnovers	Intercepts	Assists
	୲୲୲୲ ୲୲	୲୲୲୲ ୲୲୲୲୲	୲୲	୲୲୲	୲୲

Diagram 24–2. Game Chart

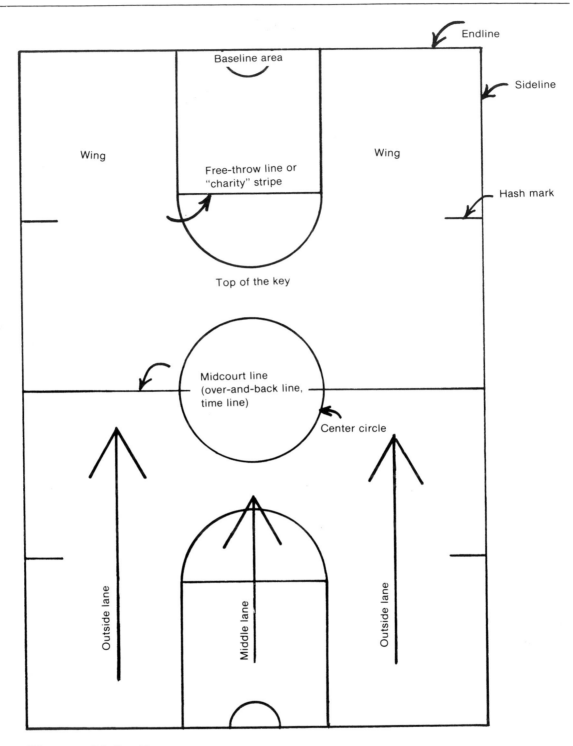

Endline

Sideline

Baseline area

Wing

Wing

Hash mark

Free-throw line or
"charity" stripe

Top of the key

Midcourt line
(over-and-back line,
time line)

Center circle

Outside lane

Middle lane

Outside lane

Diagram 24–3.　Terms

Index